A · TWODOT® · BOOK

An imprint of The Rowman & Littlefield Publishing Group, Inc.
501 Forbes Blvd., Ste. 200
nham, MD 20706
egistered trademark of The Rowman & Littlefield Publishing Group, Inc.

ributed by NATIONAL BOOK NETWORK

rary Cataloguing in Publication Information available

ongress Cataloging-in-Publication Data available

4930-3170-2 (hardcover)
4930-3171-9 (e-book)

used in this publication meets the minimum requirements of American
rd for Information Sciences—Permanence of Paper for Printed Library
NISO Z39.48-1992.

ted States of America

COLD CASE

BILLY THE KID

INVESTIGAT
HISTORY'S MYST

W. C. JAME

GUILFORD, C

British Li

Library of

ISBN 978-1
ISBN 978-1-

The paper
National Standa
Materials, ANSI

Printed in the Un

CONTENTS

FOREWORD

BY W. C. JAMESON

I first met Steve Sederwall in 2006 at a book signing in Capitan, New Mexico. The book I was doing a reading from and signing was *Billy the Kid: Beyond the Grave*, which provides powerful and compelling evidence that the famous outlaw was not shot and killed as alleged by Sheriff Pat Garrett, but lived a long, not necessarily happy, life, passing away from a heart attack in Texas on December 27, 1950. Because the contents of the book took issue with the prevailing notions about the Kid, it upset, even angered, those who professed to be experts and vigorously supported the legend. To date, while a handful of so-called authorities have argued against the findings I presented in the book, none has ever presented evidence sufficient to support their positions.

I knew Sederwall by reputation. He had generated newspaper headlines as well as television appearances relating to his aggressive investigations into a variety of Billy the Kid–related events. His findings were based on solid police work, and they differed, sometimes dramatically, from the established history laid down by writers who claimed to be historians. As a result, Sederwall was also irritating a number of self-anointed experts on the outlaw and his life and times. Sederwall ignored them all and continued with his work. I was hoping he would be at the book signing; I wanted to meet the man.

Following the signing of books, a pleasant gathering ensued with snacks and wine. I visited with the guests and engaged in conversations about Billy the Kid, Pat Garrett, and New Mexico history. Though I had never seen Sederwall before, I knew it was him the minute the crowd parted to allow this six-foot-five-inch, broad-shouldered man wearing a Stetson, a badge, and a pistol to approach. He stepped up to me, introduced himself, and confronted me on a few findings in my book with which he took issue.

Twelve years later, we still argue and disagree, but what became clear from that first meeting was that, though we have our differences, we are both interested in the same thing: the truth. We just chase it down in different ways.

I have learned a lot from Sederwall. His tenacity and thoroughness when taking on the study of historical topics is exceeded by no one I have ever encountered. I have spent more years than I care to admit in academic settings and have never encountered anyone with research and investigation abilities equal to Sederwall's. His talent for ferreting out evidence and facts long overlooked or ignored by the Billy the Kid establishment researchers is nothing short of amazing. His ability to deconstruct and analyze evidence is astounding. He is tenacious, determined, efficient, and thorough.

Steven M. Sederwall comes by all of this honestly. He has been a cop for most of his adult life. He served in police departments in Texas and California and as a criminal investigator for the United States government. He has been involved in hundreds of investigations and worked dozens of crime scenes. With every assignment he gained more experience, more expertise. After decades of law enforcement and criminal investigation adventures, he has developed a keen sense for identifying and separating evidential fact from perception and myth. As an investigator he has recorded numerous successes. Today, Sederwall operates his own investigative agency. He is a private detective, but unlike most detectives, he specializes in investigating western cold cases, decades-old crimes and mysteries that either have never been solved or were bungled. In 1998 he decided to take on a series of major cold cases related to the mishandling of the life and times of the outlaw Billy the Kid.

There are, and have been, a number of doyens who do not hesitate to inform the likes of Steve Sederwall, me, and others that a crime scene investigation, as well as other forensic applications, cannot be conducted relative to events that took place a hundred or more years ago. They are wrong. The truth is, the literature is filled with examples of investigations of decades-old, even centuries-old, events that have succeeded in bringing to light certain facts heretofore missed, and which have resulted in the presentation of new truths.

Deoxyribonucleic acid—DNA—is a genetic "fingerprint" inherited from our parents, and has proven to be a virtually irrefutable forensic investigation tool. Useful DNA has been extracted from bones and teeth millions of years old.

A variety of chemical analyses can be applied to age-old crime scenes and mysteries. It had long been suspected that President Zachary Taylor, who died in office in 1850, was a victim of arsenic poisoning. His remains were disinterred and tested, the result being that no arsenic was found. Certain chemicals can be employed to locate decades-old bloodstains invisible to the human eye.

Site analysis is another important forensic tool. All events occur in a place, and the geography of that place can provide clues as to how a situation unfolded, even determine what could have happened. While researchers and writers have examined historical events over the centuries, precious few, we have learned, actually traveled to the location of an occurrence and conducted an appropriate site analysis. Site analysis contributed to a greater understanding of the Battle of the Little Bighorn as well as the assassination of Pat Garrett.

Such tools and techniques as described above are part of Sederwall's investigation kit, and he applies them with the skill expected of a professional. His results have yielded heretofore unknown information and facts relative to selected mysteries.

"All history is mystery," says author Dale L. Walker, "and historians have not done a particularly good job of unraveling them, and in many cases misinterpret and misreport them." Matthew Arnold puts it less kindly; he insists that history is "a huge Mississippi of falsehoods." Napoleon pulled no punches when he stated that history is "fraud agreed upon."

Much of the published "history" of the outlaw Billy the Kid and the Lincoln County War is fraudulent. Research on these topics has been poorly conducted, if conducted at all. The research and associated writing has amounted not so much to a quest for the truth, but more to a desire to develop a case to support the legend as well the researcher's bias, and even to elevate one's position in the community of Billy the Kid scholars and enthusiasts. The question of how one's arguments are influenced by prejudgments has been a central methodological issue in history for decades.

Steve Sederwall is attracted to a good mystery, and the investigator in him craves to solve it. In reading the extant literature on Billy the Kid, Sederwall encountered a number of unsolved mysteries, but was also appalled, exasperated, and bothered by the incomplete and shoddy research conducted on the outlaw and related topics. It occurred to Sederwall that authors of Billy the Kid–related books and articles appeared not to research much of anything and relied mainly on repeating each other, sometimes word for word. If a crime scene or forensic investigator had turned in reports in the manner of these "historians," they would have been summarily dismissed.

Sederwall determined that the published "facts" pertaining to Billy the Kid were flawed and unsatisfactory. He concluded the people who called themselves historians were going about it the wrong way, and that their work lacked the fundamentals of any important investigation. He decided it was time to approach these historical puzzles not as a historian but as a police investigator, one without bias and one who was committed to learning the truth.

This approach is not new, nor unique to Sederwall. It has been pursued to great effect on a number of occasions. For example, Jeff Campbell, a retired twenty-year police investigator for the state of New Mexico who specialized in cold cases, applied his forensic skills to the infamous Sand Creek Massacre site. In November 1864, Colonel John Chivington led hundreds of cavalrymen to a Cheyenne Indian campground along Sand Creek in eastern Colorado. While the Indians waved white flags of surrender, Chivington ordered his men to open fire with carbine and cannon. In the end, 150 Indians were slaughtered, mostly old men, women, and children. The Sand Creek Massacre was the My Lai of its day, an embarrassing war crime exposed by honest soldiers and condemned by the United States government. Thanks to Campbell's investigations, the geography and logistics of attack and escape were ultimately determined.

Another example: A crime scene investigation that was initiated eighty-two years after the event yielded enough information to determine the cause of the fire that destroyed the Wolf House, the home of the writer Jack London. The investigation team consisted of a state criminologist, an expert in hydrocarbon and chemical fires, an arson investigator, and an authority on fire burn patterns. The investigation ruled out arson and attributed the cause of the blaze to a pile of cotton rags that had been soaked in linseed oil–based stains and varnishes. A forensic examination revealed that such rags were "capable of self-heating to flaming ignition in a few hours."

In what must be one of the oldest cases to be subjected to a forensic analysis, the mummified body of the pharaoh Tutankhamen, who died at nineteen years of age in 1323 BCE, was unearthed in 1922. It was determined that he suffered from malaria and epilepsy; had a clubfoot; and was afflicted with what today is known as Köhler disease, which can cause pain and swelling and leads to a pronounced limp. It was also learned from DNA analysis that Tutankhamen was the product of incest. As a result of the study, a number of researchers are convinced that Tut perished from complications related to malaria, although that contention is still being debated.

Sederwall has a passion for solving a mystery and for determining the truth. But rather than finding his quest for the truth praised and his findings entered into the arena of Billy the Kid specialists and made available for discussion and debate, he has been scorned and deemed a troublemaker by many who carry the torch for the status quo. Make no mistake: Sederwall's findings, based on an application of solid, professional forensic science and technique, have served to anger and annoy a number of the self-professed experts. Passionate Billy the Kid enthusiasts appear to be a reactionary lot: Sederwall's home has been the target of gunfire; he was once hauled into court by one of the rabid embracers of the status quo; and he has received death threats over the telephone.

This type of reaction is nothing new to those who follow Billy the Kid goings-on. Dr. C. L. Sonnichsen, the brilliant Harvard-educated historian, folklorist, and author, received a number of death threats when his somewhat revisionist book, *Alias Billy the Kid*, was released in 1955. The investigator and writer Frederick Bean, who shepherded a Federal Bureau of Investigation–based study on the true identity of Billy the Kid, also received deaths threats and warnings to "never set foot in New Mexico again." On the publication of my book, *Billy the Kid: Beyond the Grave*, I received threatening phone calls and letters, all of them anonymous.

Sederwall's quest for the truth is not deterred by death threats. As a former cop, he has been shot at before. His enthusiasm and devotion lie with determining and communicating facts, the facts that lead to the truth. The defenders of the outlaw's legend, those who have positioned themselves as the arbiters of all things Billy the Kid, are growing concerned because their foundation is disintegrating. But it was a foundation of their own making, one replete with incomplete and inferior research, concocted less with the mortar of truth and more with the always permeable and fragile air of ego and status focus.

Sederwall is unconcerned with the politics and pettiness of such things. Anyone who claims to be a historian is, or should be, after the truth. Sederwall's philosophy is more aligned with the notion that if we are after the truth, then we should all be involved in this quest together. Those not interested in the truth need to get out of the way before they get run over, because in the end the truth will win every time.

INTRODUCTION

Despite what the history books relate, a significant number of western events have been misinterpreted, misrepresented, and/or misreported. A number of these occurrences represent important, even dramatic mysteries. To the historical researchers who have studied and reported such events, they remain cut-and-dried, if their published writings are to be believed. Someone skilled and experienced in investigation, however, often encounters things that historians missed or misconstrued.

For example, the author Dee Brown not only found numerous discrepancies between the long-accepted "history" as it related to encounters between the United States military and American Indian tribes, he found significant manipulation of the truth, if not complete disregard for it. Further, Brown had his findings published in *Bury My Heart at Wounded Knee* (1970). The so-called history associated with these events, as we thought we understood it, was wrong.

For a century or more, many of the events surrounding the mysterious, fascinating, enigmatic, and popular outlaw Billy the Kid and the associated Lincoln County War have been perpetuated as immutable fact by the history establishment when, in fact, they were often regarded by those with professional investigative experience as cold cases. Though Billy the Kid enthusiasts arrived at conclusions that were communicated via book and article, no in-depth and professional investigations were ever undertaken. On close examination it was discerned that the research conducted by the enthusiasts was incomplete and amateurish, and generally amounted to little more than repetition.

With these cases the truth hovered behind the decades-thick façade of so-called historical research and reporting, waiting to burst forth, but was provided no opportunity. The fact remains that historians have a poor track record of solving cold cases, identifying pertinent pieces of evidence, interpreting them correctly, and communicating them properly so that they can be brought to light and have their day in court. This, as it turns out, is precisely what investigators do when bringing all observations and evidence to the fore.

During a criminal investigation the cop looks for facts. A mistaken belief among many is that fact and truth are synonymous. A fact is a statement or an observation about something that has occurred. Truth is the state or quality of being true and has to do with accuracy and integrity.

"Truth is made up of facts," said Dr. C. L. Sonnichsen, "but if we stop with the facts, we do not have the truth." The best part of history, continued Sonnichsen, "begins where the facts leave off [and] when we begin to consider *meanings*." Sometimes it takes several facts to make a truth. The problem with a great deal of historical writing is that it resembles simple bricklaying—the piling of one "fact" upon another with too little attention to the mortar that holds the structure together. Somewhere among the facts lies the truth, and it sometimes requires chipping away at the old mortar. Therein lies the excitement of discovery and connections. "The reason so much historical writing is so dull," according to Sonnichsen, "is that is has no connection with the adventure of the human spirit."

With the exception of only a handful of publications, the literature related to the outlaw Billy the Kid appears to be oriented toward perpetuating the timeworn legend. After all, it is only the legend, the myth, that most people know, not the truth. The story of the Kid has been filtered through what historians thought or believed. In the end, however, readers were spoon-fed essentially the same version of the legend over and over. Legend, as defined by *The New Lexicon Webster's Dictionary*, is "a story handed down from the past which lacks accurate historical evidence but has been popularly accepted as true."

History is, or is supposed to be, a quest for the truth. It is the historian's job to evaluate information found, analyze it, track down the provenance, form conclusions, and tender them to the public. Most of the history related to the life and times of Billy the Kid has all of the earmarks of a quest not to uncover the truth but to perpetuate the legend.

During the process of historical research and reporting, and the associated quest for truth, it serves no purpose to build barriers to keep out conflicting findings and opinions. The honest and professional approach is to invite scrutiny and to listen to other points of view, other hypotheses and conclusions. Following this, the professional historian, or anyone with any degree of integrity and honesty, will then allow opportunity for discussion and debate, all in the interest of learning the truth. When this does not take place, fraud occurs. The individuals and cliques who construct the barriers to debate and openness perpetuate the fraud. Unfortunately, this tendency characterizes much of the current paradigm of Billy the Kid–related studies.

For decades a number of people have immersed themselves in the examination of this famous outlaw. They have included academic historians, amateur historians, enthusiasts, hobbyists, and the merely curious. For the purpose of eliminating the cumbersome identification of these separate groups, in the following pages they will all be referred to as historians since the majority of them identify themselves as such, credentialed or not.

Sadly, western outlaw and lawman history is not held in high regard by most institutions of higher learning where many legitimate historians abide. These topics do not generate impressive amounts of research funding or large grants, and tend to lack prestige among academic peers. Virtually all of the periodicals associated with such topics are not academic, or even particularly professional. On the other hand, there are a handful of historians possessing academic credentials who dabble in outlaw history.

The bulk of research on and writing about Billy the Kid, therefore, has been contributed by amateur historians and enthusiasts. A thorough examination of the body of literature available on the Kid reveals that precious little competent, authoritative, or original research has ever been undertaken. There exists little to no activity beyond looking up what others have already written and simply repeating it. Even a cursory examination of the extant literature on the topic verifies this.

Unfortunately for those interested in the truth, accuracy, and professionalism that one expects to find associated with competent and sophisticated historical research, there has been a troubling absence of mature investigation involving deconstruction, analysis, reconstruction, and professional presentation. With very few exceptions it has been mostly repetition.

It is possible to construct a literary genealogy of Billy the Kid literature, with most of the published offspring ultimately linked to the 1882 publication of *The Authentic Life of Billy the Kid*. Sheriff Pat Garrett, the alleged killer of Billy the Kid, is listed as the author. During the more than a century since Garrett's book was released, it has been declared a collection of lies and misinterpretation. Writer Frederick Nolan has described it as "a farrago of nonsense" and "responsible for every single one of the myths perpetuated about Billy the Kid" and "many inaccuracies, evasions, and even untruths." History records that Garrett's friend and drinking buddy Ashmon Upson wrote most of the book.

Some argue that he may have written all of it. Whatever the case, an examination of the text causes the investigator to wonder if Pat Garrett ever actually read the book before it was published. If he had, he would never have allowed its release, because it was filled with apparent inconsistencies, contradictions, and falsehoods.

Garrett's book was misleading and in error, and that has been proven time and again. Thus, it confuses and frustrates the honest pursuer of the truth in history when it is discovered that the so-called experts on the subject of Billy the Kid have done little more than repeat what Garrett said, along with repeating each other. What possible reason could there be for this state of affairs? Respected academicians relate that it is easy to look up material and repeat it. Detailed research, investigation, deconstruction, analysis, reconstruction, and careful and accurate reporting, however, require time, energy, and hard work.

Over the years careful readings of *Authentic Life* have generated suspicions among the investigative-minded related to the truth about Billy the Kid from the time of his birth to his alleged demise at the hands of Garrett. This troubling book is not to be trusted. For decades, however, it has served as a font of information, though spurious, to undiscerning historians and writers.

According to investigator Steve Sederwall, however, *Authentic Life* contains a number of "tells." A tell is a cop term for a sign, always present, that points to the truth. In history one often encounters tells—it can be a witness testimony or a sentence or paragraph—that serve to lead one away from the truth, sometimes intentionally and sometimes accidentally. Tells are found throughout *Authentic Life*. They are also found in abundance in a book penned by Garrett's deputy, John Poe (*The Death of Billy the Kid*). Poe's book, in part, was an attempt to validate Garrett's words and claims, but because of the appearance of numerous tells, it accomplished just the opposite. Tells are also found throughout much of the literature related to Billy the Kid. The tells lead to evidence, and the evidence was not always consistent with the legend.

From the time that the outlaw Billy the Kid became a subject for research and publication, the tells, and there were dozens, slipped by the historians. Eventually, though, they were recognized and identified by Sederwall. In the following pages these tells are investigated, analyzed, and reported.

Billy the Kid was a legitimate outlaw for a number of reasons. He stole livestock, was involved in the passing of counterfeit money, and killed people. There is no need here for any attempt to sanitize the Kid's reputation. What will be shown in the following pages, however, is that the Kid was no more of an outlaw than the cast of characters who ran Lincoln County, New Mexico, and the surrounding area. This group included businessmen, politicians, ranchers, and law enforcement personnel. Their crimes, immoral yet viewed as legal, included deceit, dishonesty, manipulation, theft, bribery, terrorism, and murder. Much of the criminal activity attached to Billy the Kid was, in fact, related to his interference with the crimes of those in power—those who had the authority to declare who was an outlaw and who wasn't.

Disturbed, frustrated, and intellectually unfulfilled by the hundreds of suspect books and thousands of repetitious and shallow articles on Billy the Kid, Sederwall decided to undertake a series of projects aimed at trying to learn what actually happened. He applied police investigative techniques to the life and times of Billy the Kid, something that had never been done before. Such a process is effective, not only in law enforcement but in interpreting history as well. Additionally, after identifying a number of crime scenes involving the Kid, Sederwall chose to apply contemporary forensic and crime scene investigation techniques to the appropriate sites and situations, as well as to numerous government and other reports.

The results of his investigations troubled a lot of people—so-called Billy the Kid experts, businessmen, and politicians clear up to and including the office of the governor of New Mexico. Sederwall's findings created a panic among those who sought to preserve the Billy the Kid legend, and what they presumed were the financial benefits of such an association. At every turn attempts to thwart Sederwall's investigations were initiated by politicians, government officials, historians, writers, and others.

Sederwall's only objective has been to try to understand what really happened. Determining the truth was his sole agenda. As he learned along the way, many did not want the truth revealed: historians whose reputations were tied to Billy the Kid, businessmen who made all or part of their living trading on the outlaw's name and legend, politicians running scared from dozens of concerns voiced by voters and contributors.

Most versions of the New Testament carry a telling quote from Jesus in John (8:32): "Then you will know the truth, and the truth will set you free." When it comes to Billy the Kid, the truth, rather than set anyone free, has the potential and capacity to irritate and annoy. Sederwall discovered through experience that many are not interested in the truth. They want the legend. One of the aides to the governor of New Mexico explained to Sederwall that the legend, as it was perpetuated by state and business interests, meant tourism dollars. As a result, no one wanted the truth. They wanted money.

The following pages relate Steve Sederwall's quest for the truth. The obstacles he confronted are described, and his findings are presented straightforwardly and honestly. His quest has nettled the keepers of the Billy the Kid mythical flame, along with more politicians than Sederwall can count. The difference between Sederwall's truths and those of the "experts" who came before him is that he has the physical and cultural evidence to back them up. The historians do not.

Challenge Sederwall if you will. He appreciates a good challenge and loves a good fight. He has erected no barriers, and unlike the history cartel, he welcomes discussion and debate. If the challenge is honest and sincere, then the challenger, like him, is after the truth.

The myth of the outlaw Billy the Kid has endured for well over a century. Beneath the layers of legend, the truth has lain largely undisturbed, rarely recognized, often ignored. In peeling away the layers of myth and legend, as well as the bungled interpretations and writings, Sederwall exposes the errors and brings truth to the light. Legends are dramatic, adventurous, and romantic. That is why they are embraced. The truth, honestly, is all of that and much more. The truth provides deeper insight into this enigmatic man known as Billy the Kid, as well as his antagonists.

Those who seek to protect and perpetuate the legend have every right to do so. If they are honest and forthright, however, they will also give credence to the truth. History has shown us that honesty and forthrightness have never been paramount. Nonetheless, the truth remains a smiling challenge that will never go away.

Chapter One

THE GENESIS OF THE OUTLAW BILLY THE KID

The origins of the outlaw Billy the Kid, specifically regarding his birthplace, his parents, and where he spent his childhood, have long been written about and occasionally debated by western outlaw enthusiasts, as well as the occasional legitimate historian. Though locations as diverse as Missouri, Kansas, Texas, and elsewhere have been mentioned as the outlaw's place of birth, most writers have identified it as New York City, though not a scintilla of evidence has ever been presented to verify this. The source of that information was Sheriff Pat Garrett's book.

The Kid's natal origins are less important than the outlaw legend he was to become. The greatest number of those who profess to be experts and who have written about nineteenth-century New Mexico outlaw and lawman history generally agree that the Lincoln County War was likely the catalyst that catapulted the Kid to fame. This conflict commenced with the murder of John H. Tunstall, a rancher and the Kid's employer, on February 18, 1878, and wound down five months later on July 19 at the end of a five-day gun battle with the killing of Tunstall's business partner, Alexander McSween.

The Lincoln County War was, and remains, on a national scale somewhat obscure. For New Mexicans, however, it endures

Billy the Kid
W. C. JAMESON COLLECTION

as a seminal event and is important for a number of reasons. One of these relates to the fact that it was a struggle for economic power in a region of New Mexico where wealth was scarce, a struggle that resulted in numerous deaths and made headlines throughout the region. Another reason is that it provided a setting for the dramatic introduction to the American public of arguably the most famous outlaw in America—Billy the Kid.

Eastern novelists wrote books about the Kid, fanciful and dramatic tales that bore little to no resemblance to the truth. These dime novels, which often portrayed the youthful outlaw as daring, charming, and a kind of Robin Hood, introduced him to thousands of readers who were enthralled with the made-up adventures, further cementing his name and legendary exploits in the minds of the public in America and overseas. The legend grew, and is sustained today, but it remains only that. The following pages detail one man's efforts to cut through the layers of myth and arrive at the truth.

Chapter Two

THE GENESIS OF THE LINCOLN COUNTY WAR: THE KILLING OF JOHN HENRY TUNSTALL

As a result of politics, economics, power struggles, and greed, a series of related events in Lincoln County, New Mexico, were stirred into such a momentum that it seemed inevitable that the path would lead to confrontation and violence. It was not long in coming.

Important sources for significant income and profit in and around south-central New Mexico were few and far between during the 1870s. United States government contracts to supply provisions, mainly beef, to the scattered military posts and encampments, as well as to Indian reservations, represented a significant flow of money and large profits for those who held the contracts. Competition for these arrangements was intense, often bitter, and at times ruthless.

The most successful business enterprise dealing in these beef contracts during this time was owned by Lawrence G. Murphy. Murphy, in partnership with a succession of others, owned and operated a mercantile enterprise in Lincoln County, New Mexico, the largest in the area. He had no competitors, so he set prices as he chose. Murphy secured strong political alliances with territorial officials, US District Court officers, and the local sheriff. With lawmakers entirely on his side, Murphy squeezed huge profits from his customers, who consisted mostly of poor ranchers and farmers. Because of this potent monopoly and its political connections with men of power, there was little anyone could do about this iniquity.

Beginning in the early 1870s, Murphy was the principal contractor for a man named William Rosenthal, a member of a dominant clique of politicians known as the Santa Fe Ring. The Ring enjoyed a monopoly supplying the government with beef. In time, Murphy took on partner James J. Dolan, and the mercantile business was named the Murphy-Dolan Store. Dolan started out as Murphy's clerk and in a relatively short time earned the position of junior partner. Dolan eventually assumed ownership of the store in 1877, and it became known as J. J. Dolan and Company.

John Chisum, owner of one of the largest cattle ranches in New Mexico, was eager for some of the beef contracts but refused to do business with Rosenthal. During the process Chisum and Murphy became enemies.

John Tunstall, an Englishman, arrived in Lincoln County in November 1876. Descended from a family heavily involved in trading and mercantilism, he sought similar opportunities in the American Southwest and finally settled in Lincoln County. Coming from a business background, Tunstall had the notion of operating a store in Lincoln, and in the end decided to introduce competition to the Murphy-Dolan mercantile establishment.

Shortly after Tunstall opened his own mercantile business, Dolan determined that the Englishman represented a direct economic threat. Initially, Dolan scoffed at the idea that Tunstall would have any impact, but as time passed and Tunstall's clientele grew, Dolan decided something needed to be done to eliminate the competition.

In time, Tunstall and another Englishman, Alexander McSween, an attorney, partnered up in the Lincoln enterprise. The reasonable prices and honest business practices associated

John Henry Tunstall
PHOTO COURTESY OF *TRUE WEST* MAGAZINE

with the Tunstall Store soon earned the confidence and patronage of local residents.

In addition to competing with the store owned by Lawrence Murphy and J. J. Dolan, Tunstall soon became aligned with rancher John Chisum and, as a result, further drew the ire of Murphy. Deep bitterness between these men ensued.

In the meantime, McSween managed to frustrate and enrage Murphy over an insurance settlement. McSween, who had been hired by Murphy to collect on a policy related to the death of a former partner, refused to turn over the money. Murphy, who held great influence over Lincoln town and county law enforcement, got a court order that allowed him to seize some of the goods in the Tunstall Store as well as a herd of horses that were pastured out at Tunstall's ranch, located near the Rio Feliz forty miles southeast of Lincoln.

Tunstall learned about the impending court order. He also heard gossip that a posse consisting of forty-three deputized men from Lincoln intended to ride to his ranch, seize his livestock, and kill him and his cowhands. The rancher and businessman decided to thwart this threat and deliver the horses to Lincoln himself until the case could be settled.

On the morning of February 18, 1878, Tunstall and his ranch hands ate breakfast, rounded up the horses, and departed for Lincoln. The hands included Dick Brewer, Henry Brown, Fred Waite, Robert Widenmann, John Middleton, and a young man who went by the alias Billy Bonney and was soon to be better known as Billy the Kid. They drove nine horses from the Tunstall ranch toward Lincoln. After a mile Brown departed the group for unknown reasons. Ten miles later the party left the road to take a shortcut through the mountains. Waite, who was driving a wagon, remained on the main road.

Around this time a posse estimated to number twenty-five men arrived at the ranch and learned of Tunstall's intentions from the cook, Gottfried Gauss. J. J. Dolan told Deputy Billy Mathews to take fourteen men, chase down Tunstall, and retrieve the horses. Researchers differ on who these fourteen men were, and names put forth included Billy Morton, Pantaleón Gallegos, Samuel R. Perry, Charles Kruling, John Hurley, Manuel "Indian"

Segovia, George Hindman, Wallace Olinger, Robert Beckwith, Ramon Montoya, Thomas Green, Thomas Cochran, George Kitt, Andrew L. "Buckshot" Roberts, Charles Marshall, Jack Long, and George Davis. Tagging along with the posse were Jessie Evans, Frank Baker, and Tom Hill. It is not clear whether the three men were formal members of the posse or simply decided to accompany it. Evans was a known rustler of livestock with a violent criminal past. (Most historians and writers spelled his first name as "Jesse," but the outlaw himself signed his name as "Jessie.")

According to the subsequent federal report compiled by Agent Frank Warner Angel, as the posse was preparing to set out, Morton stated, "Hurry up, boys. My knife is sharp and I feel like scalping someone."

The Tunstall party paused long enough at Pajarito Springs to water their mounts and the horse herd and then proceeded along the trail. It was nearing sundown when they arrived at a divide and continued downhill. The trail was narrow, and men and horses proceeded single file, with Billy the Kid and John Middleton riding at the rear of the column. Up ahead, Brewer and Widenmann spotted a flock of turkeys and rode up a slope to try to shoot some for dinner. Tunstall remained with the horse herd.

From the top of the divide, Billy the Kid and Middleton spotted a number of riders approaching from the rear at a rapid pace. The Kid spurred his horse toward Brewer and Widenmann to warn them as Middleton went to alert Tunstall. As the Kid approached Brewer and Widenmann, the posse arrived at the crest of the divide. Posse members spotted the ranch hands and opened fire. The Kid, Brewer, and Widenmann rode a little farther into the woods and sought cover near the turkey roost. A few moments later Middleton joined them. Middleton said he tried to get Tunstall to join them, but the rancher appeared excited and confused.

According to author Robert M. Utley, the only witnesses to what happened next were the killers themselves: Billy Morton, Jessie Evans, and Tom Hill. Most researchers are convinced that, from their hiding place, estimated to be at least one hundred yards away and probably more, Billy the Kid, Brewer, Widenmann, and Middleton were unable to observe the events leading to Tunstall's killing.

Morton later explained to the others that he had ordered Tunstall to surrender when the rancher raised his handgun and fired two shots. In response, Morton said, he, Evans, and Hill returned fire. Two bullets struck the rancher—one in the chest and the other in the head, and he dropped from his horse, dead. Continued firing by the three posse members killed the horse.

John Middleton claimed that posse member Thomas Green told him that as Tunstall rode up to Evans, Morton, and Hill, Jessie Evans shot him in the chest. The impact of the bullet knocked the Englishman from his horse, and he landed face down on the ground. Morton then dismounted, picked up Tunstall's revolver, and shot him in the back of the head. Following this, he shot and killed Tunstall's horse.

Testimony by one Albert H. Howe to investigator Angel provided an account of the shooting witnessed by George B. Kitt. As Tunstall rode toward Billy Morton and Tom Hill, the posse members placed the butts of their rifles on their knees. Morton assured Tunstall that he would not be harmed, but when Tunstall had ridden close, both men fired. Howe stated that Tunstall had not drawn a weapon.

Subsequent testimony and reporting credited Morton's account of what occurred as the "official" version of the death of Tunstall: "Killed while resisting arrest by a posse led by a legally designated deputy sheriff of Lincoln County." Evans claimed in subsequent testimony that "he had not even been present with the posse." The nine horses Tunstall intended to deliver to Lincoln were rounded up, and they, along with the posse, returned to the Tunstall ranch.

In the dark, Billy the Kid, Brewer, Widenmann, and Middleton made their way out of the mountains. They arranged to have Tunstall's body retrieved and returned to Lincoln. None who knew Tunstall believed for one minute that the Englishman had been killed while resisting arrest. Such a thing was not in his nature. Most believed that Tunstall had been murdered by gunmen sent by the Murphy-Dolan faction.

What really happened to John Tunstall? The truth is, not a single crime scene investigation took place following the killing. The closest thing to an investigation that occurred was when federal agent Frank Warner Angel showed up in Lincoln County almost two and a half months later to interview participants in the incident. Angel, a special investigator, was sent as a representative of two federal departments—Justice and Interior—with orders to learn the truth of what had occurred. His mission was in response to inquiries and concerns expressed about one of their countrymen by the British foreign office. The Angel Report, submitted in October 1878, contained forty-three depositions sworn by active participants in the Lincoln County War.

In the report Sheriff William Brady, a Murphy-Dolan puppet, claimed his posse was forced to kill Tunstall in self-defense, stating that "while a portion of the posse were in pursuit of the party, J. H. Tunstall fired on the posse and in the return fire he was shot and killed." Though Brady formally organized the posse, he was not a member of it. In his report, and in spite of Brady's testimony, Angel stated, "These facts . . . lead me to the conclusion that John H. Tunstall was murdered in cold blood, and was not shot in attempting to resist an officer of the law."

Subsequent written history has relied heavily on the Angel Report, but few pertinent questions were ever raised. The earliest writers about the Lincoln County goings-on conducted no investigations, and their research amounted to little more than repeating what they read in this report, or what they thought was in the report. As a result, the early interpretations of the killing of John Tunstall lacked depth and manifested an appearance of having been developed with a nod to haste and efficiency instead of truth. Subsequent writers, in turn, even up to the present day, relied almost completely on what they had encountered in those early publications. Most of the published work on the Tunstall killing has left the discerning and questioning reader with the feeling that none of the writers possessed much insight into what actually happened relative to the killing of John Tunstall. It was clearly time for a proper investigation into these matters, one that was one and a quarter centuries late and long overdue. This was the kind of case that appealed to the detective instincts of Steve Sederwall.

An investigator, on obtaining witness testimony and an autopsy related to the Tunstall killing, is faced with two different versions of the event: (1) Sheriff Brady and members of the posse claimed that John H. Tunstall was shot and killed in self-defense, and (2) Tunstall's ranch hands insisted that the posse rode them down and murdered Tunstall in cold blood. Only one of these versions can be correct. The other is either a mistaken perception or a lie.

On April 22, 2005, Sederwall led a team of investigators to the Tunstall murder site. The location was miles from the associated historical marker erected by the state of New Mexico on US Highway 70. The last part of the route to this remote location was barely passable: a washed-out ghost of a road. To travel the last one hundred yards to the site required a four-wheel-drive vehicle or hiking in on foot. At the presumed spot where Tunstall fell, a sign erected by the Lincoln County Historical Society contained a brief explanation of what took place there in 1878.

Tunstall had been dead for 127 years, but Sederwall began looking for evidence. As far as is known, not a single researcher or writer had ever been to the site for other than a cursory visit, if at all. Sederwall's team carried evidence bags, cameras, metal detectors, shovels, and a GPS.

According to the published history, Tunstall was shot with both a rifle and a handgun, with wounds to the body and head. When the posse members fired on the rancher, they knew that in the woods nearby Billy the Kid and the rest of Tunstall's cowhands posed a potential threat. The normal reaction of the posse man who fired the rifle would have been to work the lever, cocking the weapon for the next shot and ejecting the spent round to the ground. There would have been no reason for him or anyone else to have paused long enough to retrieve the spent shell casing. Even though more than a century and a quarter had passed, the possibility existed that at least one spent cartridge might be found.

Sederwall's investigation team undertook a grid search, working their way from the monument up the hill toward the south. Two hours and ten minutes after arriving, one of the team members called to the others, stating that he had found something.

A spent cartridge, a rifle casing, was located with a metal detector two and a half inches deep in the ground and close to forty yards southeast of the monument. As expected, it was bent and badly rusted. Part of the front end was missing, likely decomposed via oxidation. There were no markings on the head of the casing, but it was clear that it was of a large caliber. The strike mark from the firing pin was slightly off-center. The discovery and its location were logged and the shell placed in an evidence bag. The search continued to the top of the hill, the crest from which the posse first spotted the Tunstall party in 1878. Nothing more was found.

Later that same day a weapons expert identified the casing as a ".45-.70, an old military round." It was explained that during the 1800s the United States military purchased ammunition from Europe and the specs did not require headstamps; hence the absence of information on the casing. After being told where the casing was found, the expert stated that it was likely that the military supplied the Lincoln County sheriff's department with ammunition. Fort Stanton was located eight miles west of Lincoln. It was also explained that there existed the possibility that the ammunition could have been stolen and resold.

Sederwall sent the casing to Mike Haag, a forensic firearm examiner for the Albuquerque Police Department. His report contained the information that the cartridge was consistent with a "45-70 Government (45 Government) caliber" that had been introduced around 1873. Through the late 1800s this type of cartridge was most often associated with the Springfield Model 1873 rifle, often referred to as the Trapdoor Springfield.

Could this have been the casing of the slug that killed John Tunstall? A correlative question should be: What are the likely alternative sources for such a shell casing at this location? Regarding the latter question, the only reasonable explanation for the existence of such a shell at this location would be related to hunting. A short distance from the Tunstall monument is a large turkey roost, likely the same one that attracted Brewer and Widenmann long ago, since turkeys will roost in the same location for decades. There were also signs of deer in the area. While this location affords real and potential hunting opportunities, it should be pointed out that it is a long way from other established sites that are considerably easier to access. Furthermore, if this location had been a known and established location for hunting, evidence in the form of other rifle, as well as shotgun, casings should be found. The .45-.70 casing located by the investigation team was the only one found in the entire area. This casing was correlated to the correct time period and the exact location—chronologically and geographically—and provided sufficient evidence to suggest that it likely came from a weapon that was fired at John Tunstall, one that may have killed him.

The discovery of the casing, however provocative, does not prove anything one way or another; it does not indicate whether Tunstall was murdered or shot in self-defense. To get closer to the truth, therefore, an evaluation of the autopsy was in order. As it turned out, a postmortem examination on the body of Tunstall was conducted by Lt. Daniel M. Appel, post surgeon at Fort Stanton. It reads:

> *Wounded in the head, entered 3 in. behind and in the line with the superior border of the right ear, made its exit 1½ in. above the left orbit and ¼ in. left of the middle line of the forehead.*
>
> *The wound in the chest entered 2 in. to the right of the median line, breaking the clavicle, and made its exit 3½ in. from the external border of the Acromian process and scraping the upper border of the Scapula.*
>
> *The fracture of the bones of the skull extended completely around its circumference, passing through the two wounds and extending downward through the horizontal plate of the frontal bone, the greater [illegible] of the ephinoid bone and cribuform plate of the ethmoid bone.*

Appel's report provided a window through which one can view Tunstall's wounds. It also left some clues. The first line of Appel's report provided significant information regarding how Tunstall was killed. Based on the report it was possible to arrive at different scenarios to explain the manner in which Tunstall could have received these wounds. Following an analysis of the report, along with an evaluation of witness testimony, Sederwall arrived at four different possible scenarios.

Scenario #1: On spotting the pursuing posse, Tunstall rode toward it, pulled his handgun, and fired twice. This is what Sheriff William Brady stated in his report. At this point, with Tunstall posing a threat to the lawmen, the posse members would have been justified in returning fire.

One of the posse member's bullets struck Tunstall "in the chest[,] entered 2 in. to the right of the median line, breaking the clavicle, and made its exit 3½ in. from the external border of the Acromian process and scraping the upper border of the Scapula." The clavicle and the upper border of the scapula are nearly in line. This wound would not have been immediately fatal, but could have knocked Tunstall from his saddle. On hitting the ground, the chances were good that he would have still been alive. The second shot, the one that would have most certainly ended his life, was to the back of his head, as indicated by Dr. Appel.

Had Tunstall been shot in the head as described by Appel, he would have to have been lying on the ground, face down. In this position Tunstall did not pose a threat. To shoot someone in the back of the head while they are still alive and lying face down on the ground is not self-defense; it is murder.

Scenario #2: If, as stated by Sheriff Brady, the posse fired at Tunstall in self-defense, one of the bullets could have struck the rancher in the chest as indicated by Appel. If he did not fall from the saddle but instead turned his horse and fled, his back would have been to the posse and therefore he was not an immediate threat. At this stage of the event, Tunstall was shot in the back of the head. This shot was not in self-defense, as the target was running away. This becomes murder.

Scenario #3: According to the testimony provided by Billy the Kid, the posse rode up to Tunstall. This and other testimony suggested that the rancher was confused and excited. After hesitating for a moment, Tunstall turned his horse and galloped away. While he was running, his back to the posse, he could not have been considered a threat. One of the posse members fired at him, the bullet striking him in the back of the head. Tunstall would not have survived this wound. While he was lying on the ground, presumably dead, a posse member rode up and shot him through the upper chest. Since Tunstall was running away after spotting the posse in pursuit, he could not have been legally regarded as a threat. His back was to the shooters. Thus, this constitutes murder.

Testimony from both Sheriff Brady and the members of the posse, as well as Tunstall's ranch hands, supports the notion that Billy the Kid and John Middleton were riding at the end of the column consisting of them, along with Tunstall, Brewer, and Widenmann and the nine horses they were herding. When the Kid reached the top of the divide, approximately three miles from the Rio Ruidoso, he "saw a large party of men coming toward them from the rear at full speed." The Kid and Middleton then rode down the hill shouting a warning.

This statement is confirmed by another posse man, Pantaleón Gallegos:

> *We rode about thirty miles before we came up to Tunstall and his party with the horses. Morton was ahead and the rest of us were riding behind as near as possible; there was only a trail through the mountains and it would not permit of our riding close together. Billy Morton and I first saw a man ahead riding a gray horse, who upon seeing us, called out to the men driving the horses ahead of him.*

According to testimony provided by Widenmann, Billy the Kid was riding a gray horse.

After Middleton called out to Tunstall to ride away with him, he noted that the rancher seemed to be confused. Widenmann said to him, "For God's sake, follow me!"

"What, John? What, John?" said Tunstall. These turned out to be his last words.

In the report presented by investigator Angel, he quoted Billy the Kid as stating, "The sheriff's posse was comprised of murderers, outlaws, and desperate characters, none of whom had any interest at stake in the county, nor being residents of said county."

To be aware of this, the Kid had to be close enough to the posse to recognize some or all of its members. He would have spotted Jessie Evans, a one-time partner. Evans had recently broken out of the Lincoln County jail, yet instead of being pursued and recaptured as required by law, he was armed and riding along with the sheriff's posse in plain sight.

Moments after the posse crested the divide, according to Gallegos' testimony, "Tunstall and his men left, the horses ran and scattered. Morton and John Hurley followed after." Gallegos' statement provided one of the pivotal pieces of evidence in this case.

Deputy George Hindman later told James L. Longwell that it was Morton who chased Tunstall. He said that Morton, "who was at that time in command of the posse, came up to Tunstall who was driving the horses and waived the attachment and called upon him to halt and Tunstall and his men ran and scattered and then Tunstall turned back and fired."

Gallegos was quoted as stating:

> *The next thing that occurred was my hearing shots fired in quick succession. Afterwards, Morton returned and said that a man had been shot and killed. I asked how it occurred. He said, "I rode after Tunstall telling him to halt and waving at him with the attachment. Suddenly Tunstall wheeled his horse around and came towards me on a jog trot with his hand on his revolver. I asked him to halt again, as I desired to serve a writ and to throw up his hands and he would not be hurt. In place of which he, Tunstall, pulled out his six-shooter and fired at me. Whereupon I and those with me returned fire.*

The evidence does not support the version of the event as related by Sheriff Brady. What the evidence does support, however, is that a legally organized law enforcement posse turned into a mob and, either in the excitement of the chase or as a result of previous planning, murdered John Tunstall. As a result of Sederwall's analysis of the evidence in the form of testimony, an additional scenario is possible.

Scenario #4: In addition to a long career in law enforcement and years as a private detective, Sederwall is also a competent horseman. These skills and experiences served him well in making a determination relative to yet another scenario, one likely closer to what actually happened.

Billy Morton (often called Buck by his confederates), who a short time earlier stated, "My knife is sharp and I feel like scalping someone," manifested clear intent to do harm to Tunstall. After a careful review of the crime scene, along with witness testimony, Sederwall is convinced that Morton, after spotting the rancher, rode his horse down the hill after him. As Morton gave chase, he reached down and pulled his rifle from the scabbard attached to the right side of the saddle. After pulling the rifle, he reined in his horse and stepped off the left side, holding on to the reins. The horse continued forward until reaching the end of the rein. The horse's head was pulled around until the animal was facing Morton and positioned slightly to his left. Morton raised the rifle to this shoulder, levered a round into the weapon's chamber, and stepped forward, causing his horse to step behind him. Morton sighted down on the back of the fleeing Tunstall and fired.

As Tunstall was riding away from the shooter, his horse's motion was up and down with each lunge forward. If Morton held his aim on Tunstall's back, the target would be up when the horse's front feet came off the ground and the target down when the front feet hit the ground. At that distance the target could move up and down as much as a foot from the point of aim. If Morton aimed at Tunstall's back and fired as the front feet of the horse were hitting the ground, the bullet could have struck Tunstall's head, as it did.

Sederwall explained that the wound to Tunstall's head was consistent with him being downhill and to the left of the shooter, explaining the source of Appel's observation that the bullet entered "3 in. behind and in line with the superior border of the right ear" and exited "1½ in. above the left orbit and ¼ in. left of the middle line of the forehead." Given Morton's position relative to Tunstall's, the wound was consistent with the target leaning forward in the saddle and looking slightly downward, the likely position of a man riding a horse away from danger.

When the bullet struck Tunstall in the back of the head, it drove him from the saddle. Morton cocked the rifle, the spent round spinning out of the weapon in an arc and falling to the right of the shooter, where it was found 127 years later by Sederwall's investigative team.

The shooter, Morton, or someone nearby rode down to where Tunstall lay face up on the ground. He pulled a revolver from his holster and fired into Tunstall's chest, missing center mass and striking him high.

If this was a murder, and the evidence points in that direction, it was one committed by a legally organized posse. Thus, according to Sederwall, the members of the posse would have found it necessary to cover it up. Deputy Wallace Olinger stated that he checked Tunstall's handgun and "found two loads out of it. It was reported that he had shot it off at Morton." Olinger also stated, "I heard, I think, two shots fired about this time." Olinger does not say he *saw* Tunstall shoot at Morton, but uses the words "it was reported." Who reported it? He does not say. Olinger was at the scene when the shooting took place; thus the phrase "it was reported" does not make sense. Olinger claims Tunstall fired at Morton, yet Sam Perry, another deputy, when interviewed by Angel, indicated Olinger was lying. He stated:

> *While I was laying out Tunstall I heard two or three shots. I will not be positive. I enquired what they were shooting about*

> *and they said they were shooting at that tree. There was some talk at the time that either Hill or Morton or Evans had fired off Tunstall's pistol. I thought it was a little strange that they were shooting at a mark. I did not think it was an appropriate time to be shooting at a mark.*

Olinger and Perry cannot both be correct. One of them is lying, and the evidence suggests that Olinger was the liar. It is not possible to be within two miles of gunfire in that particular canyon and not be aware of it. The shots were fired while Perry was tending to Tunstall's body. Olinger was aware of this and knowingly gave false testimony, a second-degree felony.

Olinger's testimony was very likely an attempt to cover Morton and back the claim of self-defense, thus providing for what lawmen call a "good shooting."

It would indeed be unreasonable to believe that Hill or Morton or Evans would be taking the time for target shooting immediately after what had just transpired. Because of the excitement related to this unfolding drama, Perry likely did not understand at the time that someone was fabricating evidence. Morton needed to have two spent rounds found in Tunstall's handgun in order to justify a claim of self-defense. Either Perry was an honest man among others of questionable character or he was not informed of the strategy employed to cover up the murder. He was upset that someone was taking target practice with the victim's handgun only minutes after the killing. Thus, the evidence shows that Hill, Morton, or Evans, or all three, intentionally perjured themselves in order to cover up the murder of John Tunstall.

There is more. John Hurley, who along with Morton chased after Tunstall, attempted to put some distance between him and the murder. In his statement Hurley said, "I was not present when Tunstall was shot. I did not see him shot. Nor did I see anyone shoot him." Clearly Hurley was trying to dispute Gallegos' statement that he and Morton went after the Englishman and did not want to be seen as a participant in the killing.

Hurley provided a tell when he tried too hard to provide denial. He stated, "If anyone says I was with any person at the immediate time of shooting Tunstall they are mistaken. I did not see his body nor did I go and look at it. I helped to attend to the horses and helped take them back to camp." Hurley's statement suggests that members of the posse were talking to one another in an effort to get their stories straight, but were too late. Gallegos had apparently already given his statement, and Hurley had been placed in the position of having to deny what was said.

Hurley would have everyone believe that he did not go look at the body. According to Sederwall, experienced law enforcement officers, no matter how many killings they might have seen, always take a look at the latest. It is human nature. Hurley was present at the shooting of Tunstall and most likely witnessed it. His statement that he did not see the body could only be a lie.

In denying that he saw anything, Hurley offered the investigator another tell that he was trying to float a lie. Instead of merely stating that he did not see the shooting, he elected to go into great detail. To the investigator, he appeared to offer too much detail. Hurley then provided himself with an alibi by saying he went to attend to the horses and took them back to camp. All of this represented a strong attempt by Hurley to put distance between himself and the murder. He, along with the other deputies, knew this was a bad shooting and that they needed to cover up the facts to make it appear justifiable.

Judge Gonzales may also have been involved in the cover-up. He stated, "On examination we found . . . that a rifle or carbine bullet had entered [Tunstall's] breast and a pistol bullet entered the back of his head coming out of the forehead." Since both bullets passed completely through the target and were unrecovered at the time, and both would have been either a .44 or .45, it would have been impossible to determine which was a handgun round and which was a rifle round.

In his report federal agent Frank Angel disputed Sheriff Brady's testimony. Angel said, "They came up to Tunstall and his party with the horses and commenced firing on them. Immediately Tunstall and his party left the horses and attempted to escape—were pursued and Tunstall was killed some hundred yards or more from the horses." At the time Angel, after reviewing all of the testimony and evidence at hand, regarded the episode as a murder.

The Lincoln County grand jury convened on April 13, 1878, and returned a true bill against Jessie Evans, Frank Rivers (an alias for Jack Long), George Davis, and Manuel Segovia, charging them with the murder of John Henry Tunstall. Curiously, Morton was not mentioned. On July 2, Robert Widenmann testified before Judge Warren Bristol that Jessie Evans was a member of the party that killed Tunstall, though he did not actually see the shooting.

When Jessie Evans was called to testify, he denied being part of the sheriff's posse that went in pursuit of Tunstall and claimed that he was more than twenty-five miles away at the time of the killing.

Up until now, all published treatments of the killing of John H. Tunstall have been incomplete, erroneous, and lacking depth. Given a close examination of the extant literature on the subject, it is clear that, other than repeating what had been previously written by others, little to no professional research and investigation were ever applied to the event until Sederwall initiated a forensic probe into the affair.

From the evidence found by investigator Sederwall in the field, along with an examination of the setting and its related geography, as well as a critical examination and analysis of the written testimony, the following can be concluded:

1. John H. Tunstall was murdered.
2. William Morton was likely the murderer.
3. The members of the sheriff's posse involved in the killing of Tunstall were aware that the killing of Tunstall was unlawful.
4. The members of the sheriff's posse, as well as the sheriff and possibly others, lied in an overt attempt to cover up their criminal act by pleading a case of self-defense.

Chapter Three

THE LAW GETS IN THE WAY OF THE TRUTH

The aftermath of the John Henry Tunstall killing turned out to be a parade of lies and attempts at covering up the illegal activities of the Lincoln County sheriff's posse. Because of loose talk from several of the posse members, only a short time passed before a surprisingly large number of Lincoln residents learned what had actually taken place.

One day after the murder, an "official" investigation was undertaken. Billy the Kid, Dick Brewer, and Robert Widenmann were interviewed. They pointed out that their first response to the murder was not to react in kind by shooting back at the attackers, but to return to Lincoln in order to provide sworn statements to Justice of the Peace John B. Wilson and allow the legal system to take its course. An early problem was encountered when the initial response by the Lincoln County sheriff's department was to lie and cover up aspects of the murder.

Wilson issued eighteen arrest warrants for posse members, including Buck Morton, Jessie Evans, J. J. Dolan, and Sheriff William Brady. The warrants were delivered to Constable Atanacio Martinez, who, in turn, deputized Fred Waite and Billy the Kid to assist him with serving them on Sheriff Brady and his deputies. When Martinez, Waite, and the Kid arrived at J. J. Dolan's store, Sheriff Brady and a handful of deputies confronted the trio, disarmed them, and had them arrested. The three were charged with "riot."

Assigning a charge of "riot" suggested the level of desperation felt by Brady, who was well aware that the killing of Tunstall was a bad shooting and that his deputies had violated the law. The statute books of the time defined riot as when "three or more persons shall assemble together with the intent to do any unlawful act." The fact remained that Constable Martinez, an elected official, had formally deputized the Kid and Waite, thus providing them with the legal status of lawmen. Any "intent to do any unlawful act" cannot be demonstrated, and nothing unlawful regarding their presence can be proven. In fact, Constable Martinez was bound by law to serve the warrants given him by Justice Wilson. Failure to do so would have been considered a felony. Martinez was indeed acting properly and within the bounds of law; Sheriff Brady was not.

If Brady had arrested Martinez during the latter's attempt to serve the warrants, he would have been in violation of "resisting an officer," a Territorial Act passed on February 15, 1854. The act reads, "If any person shall resist or abuse a judge, justice of the peace, sheriff, constable, or other officer in the execution of his office . . ." Thus, the law did not exempt Brady from arrest, nor did it provide him any leeway in obstructing Martinez in the execution of his duty.

Brady allowed himself to be arrested and was held on a two-hundred-dollar bond. Later he bonded out and then proceeded to arrest Martinez, Waite, and the Kid on the trumped-up charge of riot.

Brady knew well that the charge of riot was a stretch. As events developed, it turned out that the sheriff was not beyond further lies. In a March 4, 1878, letter to District Attorney W. L. Rynerson, Brady tried to cover up the activities of the posse. He claimed that Tunstall attempted to run with the horses that the posse was legally bound to impound and then stated that "J. H. Tunstall fired on the posse," in an attempt to justify the homicide. Brady knew he was in trouble when in the same letter he stated: "It is falsely averred that attached to my deputy's posse were men against whom U. S. warrants had been issued. To disprove this, I present you a letter which reached [Mathews] before he attached, and in addition to my minute verbal instructions."

The letter attached by Brady, dated February 15, 1878, is addressed to J. B. "Billy" Mathews, Deputy Sheriff, and reads:

> *Dear Sir,*
>
> *You must not by any means call on or allow to travel with your posse any person or persons who are known to be outlaws. Let your Mexicans round up the cattle and protect them with the balance. Be firm and do your duty according to law and I will be responsible for your acts.*
>
> *I am sir, respectfully yours,*
>
> *William Brady, Sheriff, Lincoln Co.*

According to Sederwall, Brady's letter is a lie. Furthermore, he says, the copy of the letter to Deputy Mathews possesses all of the earmarks of having been written *after* the fact, an attempt to remove the sheriff from any wrongdoing. According to several statements made by posse members, Jessie Evans and Tom Hill were among the group that went to Tunstall's ranch to secure the livestock, and the other posse members knew exactly who and what they were—known outlaws. Evans and Hill, who had only a short time earlier escaped from jail, accompanied Brady's legal posse. Brady was attempting even more cover-up.

Why would the sheriff feel it was necessary to tell his own deputy not to commit a felony? The belief that Brady was lying was held by others at the time. J. H. Koogler, the editor of the *Las*

Vegas Gazette, had been provided a copy of the letter Brady wrote to District Attorney Rynerson. In response to the letter, Koogler wrote, in part:

> *Why did Sheriff Brady find it necessary to instruct his deputy not to select "known outlaws" as a posse? Why did he permit a man to act as his deputy to whom it was necessary to send such instructions? And how did it come that notwithstanding the sheriff's written order, we find these "known outlaws" not only traveling and acting with the posse, but brutally murdering Tunstall under cover of the deputy sheriff's authority? These are matters which must be cleared up.*

Brady was in violation of the law, and he knew it. When his deputies did not arrest Evans and Hill, they were in violation of "Allowing to Escape by Failing to Execute Process," which occurred when the lawmen failed "to apprehend or confine any person convicted or charged with an offense."

Brady claimed that Evans and Hill did not ride with the posse. Posse members are on record as stating that the two outlaws were members of the group. Someone was lying, and the obvious conclusion is that it was the sheriff, William Brady.

The available evidence supports a charge of murder against the Lincoln County deputies and the noncommissioned members of the posse. Charges against these men and others who further compounded the crime by providing false statements and tampering with evidence could have been filed and should have been filed, but they were not. Even though Sheriff William Brady was not present when John Tunstall was murdered, it is evident from the statements provided by his posse that the case against the sheriff for conspiring to cover up a capital crime must have been made.

Chapter Four

REVENGE

Though businessman and rancher John H. Tunstall was detested by James J. Dolan, Lawrence Murphy, and Sheriff William Brady, he was well respected by the men who worked for him on his ranch, including Billy the Kid, Fred Waite, Robert Widenmann, and Dick Brewer. By all accounts Tunstall was a good man; he was good to his employees and dealt with them honestly and decently. Regarding his employer, Billy the Kid stated, "He had been good to me and treated me like a gentleman. I lost the best friend I ever had when they killed him." Billy the Kid regarded Tunstall as a fine man and was saddened by his killing. He swore he would make the members of Brady's posse pay with their lives.

While a part of Billy the Kid may have held out the hope of exacting justice, it is likely that he was just as interested, if not more so, in revenge. Events that occurred during the following days would tend to make his motivation clear.

Dick Brewer knew a judge who might be willing to help bring Tunstall's killers to justice. Brewer proposed that he and the Kid visit Justice Wilson, identify the men who were witnesses to the Tunstall murder, and seek justice. On March 1, 1878, Wilson appointed Brewer as a special constable and provided him with warrants to arrest members of Brady's posse. Brewer deputized the Kid, Fred Waite, Henry Brown, Charlie Bowdre, Frank McNab, and a few others. The group was known as the

Regulators. The following day the Regulators, eleven of them, set out to search for the murderers of Tunstall. On March 6 they spotted a party of five horsemen near the Rio Peñasco and recognized some of the killers. As the Regulators rode toward them, they were spotted, and their quarry split up into two groups. The Regulators pursued three men they recognized and had warrants for: Billy Morton, Frank Baker, and Dick Lloyd (some researchers identify him as Sam Lloyd).

In the minds of many, Morton was the man who shot and killed John Tunstall. Morton, originally from Virginia, was known to have killed at least three men prior to arriving in Lincoln County. Frank Baker was described in the book *History of the Lincoln County War* by Maurice G. Fulton, quoting Ashmon Upson, as one "who shot innocent men when they were on their knees, pleading for life. With a brutal laugh [Baker] held a pistol to their heads, and after blowing their brains out, kicking the inanimate body and face to jelly." Little is known about Dick Lloyd.

For the next five miles, a running gun battle ensued until Lloyd's horse gave out and stumbled, throwing Lloyd from the saddle. Lloyd jumped up and raised his hands in surrender, but the Regulators rode past him, their sights set on Morton and Baker. The poor horses ridden by the two fleeing men soon grew exhausted and refused to go any farther. Seeing their escape thwarted, Morton and Baker surrendered to Brewer's posse. Billy the Kid wanted to kill the two men where they stood, but Brewer calmed him down and explained that they had a responsibility to return them to Lincoln.

On the evening of March 8, the Regulators, with Morton and Baker their prisoners, stopped at John Chisum's South Spring Ranch, where they were joined by William McCloskey. Brewer distrusted McCloskey, who was a good friend of Morton. McCloskey, according to some researchers, had been a member of Morton's posse that overtook Tunstall. At Chisum's ranch Morton wrote a letter to a cousin in Richmond, Virginia, explaining his predicament and his fear that he would be killed. Midmorning of the following day, the Regulators stopped at the Roswell post office, where Morton posted his letter. He told Postmaster Ashmon Upson that he believed his captors were going to kill him. William McCloskey, riding with the Regulators, assured Upson that the prisoners would arrive in Lincoln alive.

On leaving Roswell, the Regulators followed the seldom used Military Road to Lincoln, hoping to avoid any encounter with other members of Brady's posse. Along the way the party stopped to camp for the night near Agua Negra Spring. As it was nearing sundown, McCloskey, Morton, and Baker were shot and killed. To this day, the shootings remain controversial, and what little that has been written about the affair comes from testimony of the Regulators who were present and the opinions of others who had a vested interest. There exist several conflicting versions of what took place. The only investigation ever made of the crime scene was conducted by investigator Steve Sederwall and took place on July 26, 2006, 128 years after the event.

Agua Negra Spring
PHOTO COURTESY OF JULIE CARTER

According to Regulator Frank McNab, Billy Morton snatched McCloskey's handgun from his holster and shot him dead. Morton and Baker then turned their horses and attempted to escape. They were pursued, overtaken, and killed. The bodies were left where they fell. According to author Robert M. Utley, Dick Brewer told the same story to Alexander McSween on returning to Lincoln. Brewer also related the same version to his friend Frank Coe.

According to Dolan, a sworn enemy of Tunstall, the Regulators killed McCloskey "because he openly declared himself a protector of the prisoners." He also contended that Morton and Baker were shot to death while they were on their knees, hands tied behind their backs, and begging for their lives.

A man named Lucius Dills, referring to Morton and Baker, made the claim that "Opportunity was afforded me for viewing those graves in 1885 [and the] physical facts do not fit any of the varied and fantastic tales told as to the manner of their taking off." According to Dills, the two prisoners did not die while running away on horseback, but he provided no details.

Pat Garrett claimed that, unknown to Billy the Kid, three members of the Regulators decided they were going to kill Morton and Baker before reaching Lincoln. He stated that as they were nearing Agua Negra Spring, Frank McNab placed his handgun to McCloskey's head and said, "You are the son of a bitch who's got to die before harm can come to [Morton and Baker]" and fired as he spoke. Garrett said that at the shooting, Morton and Baker rode away as fast as they could.

Billy the Kid and Charlie Bowdre were riding at the head of the party. At the sound of the gunshot, the Kid spotted Morton and Baker escaping and gave chase. The Kid, according to Garrett, fired two shots from his speeding horse, killing both Morton and Baker. Garrett claims the bodies of the three dead men were found later by Mexican sheepherders, who buried them.

Agua Negra Spring is found today on a ranch owned by John Cooper. The trail to the springs winds through a rough, rocky, cactus-studded landscape and requires a four-wheel-drive vehicle. On July 26, 2006, Steve Sederwall led an investigative team to the Morton-Baker killing site to conduct a search for evidence. The team covered an area from the springs to the place where Morton and Baker were buried.

The crime scene investigation team found a number of spent cartridges fired from a rifle, along with several rounds fired from a pistol. At one location the crew found a rifle round, and then another one a step or two forward, suggesting that the shooter fired a shot, advanced, and fired again as he was working the lever of the rifle.

In all, the team found the following casings and made deductions about what kind of weapons they were fired from:

Number	Caliber	Weapon (estimated)
2	.45-.60	Winchester
4	.45	Colt
1	.38	.38 Special
1	.38	.38 Long Colt
25	.44-.40 & .45	.44-.40s (Winchester), .45s (Colts)

Regarding the version of the killing of McCloskey provided by Regulators Frank McNab and Dick Brewer, two men who were at the scene at the time of the killings, they left the impression of having been prepared ahead of time and rehearsed. In truth, however, there was little to no logic in their assessments of what transpired. McCloskey was the only member of the group who possessed a shred of empathy for the two captives, having had a long-standing friendship with Morton. Why would Morton kill the only man in the party who could possibly stand between them and death? That made no sense.

Garrett's version of the killing of McCloskey by Frank McNab carried with it more logic, but Garrett, who was not present at the killings, never explained how he came by his information. Given Garrett's proven penchant for stretching the truth, the possibility exists that his statement was a product of his imagination.

J. J. Dolan's version of the affair is troubling for two reasons. First of all, he was *not* at the scene and could not possibly have known what transpired. Second, his version of the killing of Morton and Baker was too similar to Ash Upson's description of how Frank Baker killed some of his victims to be comfortable. Ash Upson was a good friend of Pat Garrett, who, in turn, was a good friend of Dolan.

The statement by Lucius Dills, if true, supports Dolan's contention. But no details were available. Did Dills dig up the bodies and examine them? What could he have possibly discerned from the bodies, which had been underground for seven years? What were his qualifications for making such an analysis? It must also be pointed out that Dills was a good friend of Pat Garrett. In the final analysis, Dills's contentions remain suspect.

So, what really happened? Following is a reconstruction of the event based on Sederwall's CSI investigation and an analysis of the available evidence.

As the Regulators rode down the Military Road toward Agua Negra Spring, the two prisoners, Morton and Baker, were in the middle of the group to minimize any chance of escape. Common sense, as well as standard law enforcement procedure, dictates this.

Nearing Agua Negra Spring, the Regulators and their prisoners were far from the main road and any settlement or ranch house. If they planned on killing their prisoners, this would have been an ideal place to do so.

If this is what they had in mind, then in a fashion they were planning to do almost exactly what Sheriff Brady's posse did to Tunstall. Some light can be shed on this plan from a statement Billy the Kid later made to George Coe. He said, "Of course you know, George, I never meant to let them birds reach Lincoln alive." This suggests premeditated murder.

It has also been reported that the hands of Morton and Baker were tied behind their backs. If true, then it would have been difficult to impossible for Morton to have snatched McCloskey's handgun and shot him, as suggested by Frank McNab. Furthermore, it would have been difficult to execute an escape on horseback if the prisoners had been bound in this manner. The notion that the prisoners' hands were bound lacks substance.

Despite the conflicting versions of what took place, the Agua Negra incident possessed all of the earmarks of an execution. Lending credence to the execution interpretation is an article that appeared in the *Santa Fe New Mexican* on May 4, 1878. The article stated that the bodies of both Morton and Baker each manifested eleven bullet holes, one for each member of the band of Regulators.

The evidence provides for the notion that the killing of Morton and Baker was motivated by revenge, and that Billy the Kid was a principal participant.

Chapter Five

THE EVOLUTION OF AN OUTLAW

Billy the Kid as a notorious outlaw is a manufactured concept. The truth is, the Kid was little more than one of several small-time cattle and horse thieves whose rustling netted him only a small amount of intermittent income. He killed no fewer, and probably no more, than four or five men. For the most part he worked on ranches, notably those of John Chisum and John Henry Tunstall. The Kid, as a cattle thief, was known to many in southern New Mexico and the Texas Panhandle, along with a number of other troublesome rustlers.

The Kid's notoriety and fame as an outlaw initially came about from two sources: Sheriff Pat Garrett and authors of dime novels that were growing popular in the eastern United States. Garrett wrote and spoke of the Kid as if he were the scourge of the land and represented a dangerous threat. Garrett, a politician and constant self-promoter, was prone to exaggeration. If Sheriff Garrett could convince the voting populace that Billy the Kid was evil incarnate and provided a threat to men, women, children, and livestock, it would help establish him, Garrett, as the hero, the knight invincible going against the dragon. In the book that carries his name as author, *The Authentic Life of Billy the Kid*, Garrett attributed traits related to gunmanship and violence to the young outlaw to the degree that the Kid came to represent a dire threat in the minds of many that never, in truth, existed. At the very least, Garrett exaggerated, but it is more likely that he lied. Remember, Garrett had designs on running for office again, was a consummate politician, and as such he was practiced at saying what he thought people wanted to hear, and more precisely what he wanted them to hear, much as politicians do today. It was not beneath Garrett to lie in order to achieve his goals.

During the 1880s a series of dime novels was released that provided readers with a variety of hair-raising adventures and derring-do attributed to Billy the Kid, not a single one of which was true. Billy the Kid as we know him via film, novel, and a great number of alleged historical treatments is a myth. The real outlaw was someone quite different.

Formally, Billy the Kid was deemed an outlaw as a result of the stroke of a pen by then New Mexico governor Samuel Axtell, a close associate with Murphy and Dolan. In a proclamation addressed "To the citizens of Lincoln County" and issued on March 9, 1878, Axtell stated:

> *The disturbed condition of affairs at the county seat brings me to Lincoln County at this time. My only objective is to assist good citizens to uphold the laws and keep the peace. To enable all to act intelligently it is important that the following facts should be clearly understood.*
>
> *1st*
>
> *John B. Wilson's appointment by the County Commissioners as a Justice of the Peace was illegal and void and all processes issued by him were void and said Wilson has no authority whatever to act as Justice of the Peace.*

2nd

The appointment of Robert Widenmann as U. S. Marshal has been revoked, and said Widenmann is not now a peace officer nor has he any power or authority to act as such.

3rd

The President of the United States upon application by me as Governor of New Mexico has directed the Post Commander Col. George Purlington to assist Territory civil officers in maintaining order and enforcing legal process. It follows from the above statements that there is no legal process in this case to be enforced, except the writs and the processes issued out of the Third Judicial Court by Judge Bristol and there are no Territorial civil officers here to enforce these except Sheriff Brady and his deputies.

Now, therefore, consideration of the premises, I do hereby command all persons to immediately disarm and return to their homes and usual occupations under penalty of being arrested and confined in jail as disturbers of the public peace.

It is important here to look into the genesis of Axtell's proclamation. Approximately two years earlier, on April 21, 1876, Axtell visited Lawrence Murphy in Lincoln. Murphy was in business with James J. Dolan, and the two were bitter enemies of John Tunstall. During this trip, according to federal investigator Frank Angel, Axtell received a loan of $2,000 from Murphy, an amount over half of the governor's $3,500 annual salary. This exchange of money established a strong connection between the Murphy contingent (often referred to as the House of Murphy) and the office of the governor. It should also be pointed out here that Axtell had once been the governor of Utah and was removed from that position for corruption. The evidence suggests that he did not learn anything from the experience.

Sixteen days after Constable Martinez, Billy the Kid, and Fred Waite attempted to arrest the killers of John Tunstall, Murphy and Dolan decided to call in their marker on the loan to Axtell. On March 9, the same day McCloskey, Morton, and Baker were killed, making it clear that the heat was on members of Brady's posse, Governor Axtell issued his proclamation, which painted one element of the Lincoln County troubles as outlaws. Axtell's statement that Justice of the Peace Wilson's appointment was "illegal and void" automatically nullified the warrants issued on Sheriff Brady and his posse members.

Section 40, Chapter 1 of the Acts of the Legislative Assembly of the Territory of New Mexico, 22nd session, reads, in part:

> *In the event of any vacancy in any county office now existing or which may hereafter occur in any county or in any precinct or demarcation in any county, by reason of death, resignation, removal or otherwise, the county commissioners of said county shall have power to fill such vacancy by appointment until an election can be held as now provided by law.*

Under the authority of this act, the Lincoln County Commissioners named John B. Wilson to the office of justice of the peace that had recently been vacated by James H. Farmer. Thus, Governor Axtell's move to void Wilson's appointment was, in itself, illegal. Axtell had to be aware of this law, since he was territorial governor from July 30, 1875, until September 4, 1878, when he was removed from office by President Rutherford B. Hayes. The act was passed and signed by Axtell himself. Axtell willingly and knowingly circumvented the law, a law he placed on the books. It was a clear attempt to remove all law enforcement authority from everyone save for the killers themselves. The question is why?

One possible, and likely, answer is that it was the manner in which Axtell was able to repay his debt to the House of Murphy. The governor was not only circumventing the law, he was also clearly hindering the efforts to apprehend Tunstall's killers by taking away the warrants and the authority of anyone who could serve them.

The murder warrants for the Lincoln County deputies were signed by the legally appointed Judge Wilson and handed to Constable Martinez. When Martinez deputized Billy the Kid and Fred Waite on February 21, 1878, to assist in the arrest of the deputies, Martinez was well within his legal authority, and the Kid and Waite were operating legally according to the law.

During Fred Angel's investigation of the goings-on in Lincoln County, he sent Governor Axtell a set of interrogatories: questions the governor was required to answer. From the tone of the questions, it was clear that Lincoln County had become a primary focus in Washington, DC.

Angel's first question was: "What official action have you taken to quiet the troubles in Lincoln County. Please give full particulars. Attach copies of all proclamations." Angel followed this question up with another: "Under what law, by what authority and under whose advice did you issue proclamation of March 9, 1878?" Angel appeared to be aware that the governor's proclamation was illegal.

Because Angel had been interviewing citizens of Lincoln and knew the governor was showing partiality to the Murphy-Dolan cartel, he asked Axtell: "Did you consult with and listen to both sides of the Lincoln County troubles or did you not act simply on the reports brought you by what is called the 'Murphy Party' without giving what is called the 'McSween Party' a chance to be heard?"

Prior to questioning Axtell, Agent Angel had apparently uncovered information that the governor had been bought off.

One of his questions was: "Were you not at the time, just before then, or now indebted to either L. G. Murphy, J. J. Dolan or Riley in the sum of two thousand dollars or thereabouts for money loaned you?" Already knowing the answer, Angel's follow-up question was: "Have you paid them or either of them said sum? How did you pay them? When did you pay them?"

Angel, who also learned that convicted outlaw Jessie Evans rode with the sheriff's posse when Tunstall was murdered, asked the governor: "Did you not consider it an anomaly for noted outlaws to be called upon to enforce law and order?"

It was clear that Angel realized he was dealing with a corrupt politician, a territorial governor who became, in truth, a major contributing element to the problems in Lincoln County.

Perhaps the most interesting question was number twenty-six: "Do you not know that by your proclamation of March 9, 1878 you assumed the powers of the judiciary and made persons who were or had enforced the warrants of Justice Wilson outlaws?" Note that Angel said, "Do you not know . . .?" He did not say, "Do you think?" Angel was, in fact, telling the governor, in the form of a question, that his illegal actions made Billy the Kid and the rest of the Regulators officially outlaws from that point on.

Since enthusiasts and the occasional legitimate historian first began writing about the outlaw Billy the Kid decades ago, none of them ever provided this information relating to the formal genesis of the youth as an outlaw. Up until Governor Axtell's proclamations, the Kid was a minor character in the goings-on in Lincoln County and the Texas Panhandle. Rather than probe for facts and attempt to uncover the truth, as any competent investigator would be inclined to do, they simply followed the already set mythical trail.

Chapter Six

BLOOD AND MUD

A pivotal event of the Lincoln County War was the killing of Sheriff William Brady. It was pivotal because a major law enforcement figure, one who was tightly connected to the Murphy-Dolan Ring and who did their bidding, became a casualty.

The event was also critical in the evolving reputation and notoriety of the man who would become known as Billy the Kid, who was charged with the crime, subsequently arrested, tried, found guilty, and sentenced to hang, thus generating a sequence of dramatic events that were guaranteed to expand and color what was soon to become a prominent southwestern, and subsequently American, outlaw legend that became known around the world.

Because of the above-stated reasons, historians and writers have seen fit to place a level of importance on this event and consequently have included Brady's murder in all of the hundreds of books and consequential articles relating to Billy the Kid. Unfortunately, according to investigator Steve Sederwall, all of them got it wrong.

A typical, and generally accepted, version of what happened was provided by writer Frederick Nolan in his book *The Lincoln County War: A Documentary History*. In this book Sheriff Brady, along with deputies Billy Mathews, George Hindman, John Long, and George Peppin, "walked from the Dolan Store at the west end of [Lincoln] to the building which served as a courthouse, an adobe building located back from the road near the Montano Store."

Standing near the adobe wall of the corral behind the Tunstall Store, several men lay in wait, weapons in hand. While complete agreement does not exist, these men were reported to be Regulators and are variously identified as Jim French, Fred Waite, Henry Brown, Frank McNab, John Middleton, and Billy the Kid. Robert Widenmann is sometimes included in this list. Yet another account provides for the presence of two black men in the corral with the Regulators—George Washington and Severin Bates. As the Brady party came into view, shots were fired from the corral. Brady was killed immediately, "hit in the head and left side" and "riddled with balls." Hindman was struck by a single bullet. He staggered a few steps toward the courthouse and fell to the ground, dying a few moments later. Long, Peppin, and Mathews raced for cover.

Billy the Kid and Jim French jumped over the corral wall and walked toward Brady's body. The Kid was observed bending over the sheriff's corpse, apparently intent on retrieving something. History is unclear as to exactly what he was doing. Some writers have claimed he was searching Brady's body for warrants the sheriff carried for Alexander McSween. Others insist the Kid was retrieving a rifle carried by Brady, one that had been seized by the sheriff from the young outlaw a few weeks earlier. Yet another version has the Kid attempting to recover a revolver that Brady had taken from him earlier.

As the Kid and French stood in the street over Brady's body, Mathews shot at them from cover. The bullet struck the Kid on the inside of the left thigh near the buttocks, passed through the flesh, and struck French in the thigh. The two men fled from the scene, leaving Brady and Hindman lying dead in the street.

April 1 1878
County of Lincoln Territory of New Mexico

1	Pocket Watch	Silver
2	5 dollar pcs	Gold
3	2 bits	
1	Spurs	
1	Colts	No [illegible]
1	Winchester	No [illegible]
1	Pistol Scabbard With Knife	
1	Lodge Ring	
1	Keys	

The Lincoln County inventory of Sheriff Brady's property in his possession at the time of his killing
PANHANDLE PLAINS MUSEUM

Nothing found in any of the extant treatments of Billy the Kid and the Lincoln County War by Nolan and others have suggested that any kind of investigation, deconstruction, analysis, and reconstruction ever took place relative to the shooting of Sheriff Brady and Deputy Hindman. All that has been offered was the repetition of incomplete and misinterpreted presentations of what others had written, and as it turns out, it appears that little of it came close to being the truth.

Following a thorough examination of the available testimony, a thoughtful and professional analysis of the crime scene, and an application of investigative logic, Steve Sederwall arrived at the following representation of what most likely occurred.

Early on the day of the ambush, April 1, 1878, Sheriff Brady had ridden into Lincoln from his residence five miles east of town. He rode directly to the courthouse. On his way to town, Brady guided his horse along a muddy, slippery road. A heavy rain, accompanied by snow, had fallen most of the night. It had rained so hard that Alexander McSween, his wife, John Chisum, and Montague Richard Levinson, traveling to Lincoln to attend court the next morning, were forced to halt at a ranch ten miles south of town.

By the time Brady arrived in Lincoln, the rain and snow had ceased. The morning was overcast and cold. Water ran deep in the arroyos, and corrals were mud-filled. The main street of Lincoln was muddy and pocked with standing puddles of rainwater. At the edge of the road, runoff coursed down the shallow grade.

Brady was expecting a busy day with a full court docket. On arriving, he learned from his clerk that the session of the district court had actually been scheduled a week later, for April 8, but due to a misunderstanding had been announced for April 1. Brady was now in the position of having to move about Lincoln posting notices informing citizens of the change in schedule. Brady ordered his clerk to draft the notices to be hung. While this was being done, Brady mounted his horse and rode down a muddy street west to the Wortley Hotel, where he ordered breakfast.

Following his meal, Brady decided to go across the street to the Murphy-Dolan Store. Because the street was so muddy, he untied his horse, climbed into the saddle, and rode the few yards to the other side of the road. After conducting whatever business he intended at the store, he remounted his horse and, joined by Mathews, Peppin, Hindman, and Long, set out down the street toward the east. The wind had picked up, and it was sleeting.

If Brady was going to be involved only with tacking up notices down the street, why was it necessary to be accompanied by four deputies? It must be remembered that since the Tunstall killing, men on both sides of the issue traveled in packs out of self-defense. There was, they hoped, safety in numbers.

At that moment Billy the Kid and some companions, most of them alleged to be Regulators, were huddled in the corral near the Tunstall Store. Some claim the men were simply hanging out; others insist they were lying in wait for the sheriff. Some have postulated that the Kid had set out to kill Brady in retaliation and revenge for the Tunstall murder, and had found a suitable place to do so. According to an interview with Francisco Trujillo found in the National Archives, Alexander McSween had told the Kid, "As soon as I arrive [in Lincoln], Brady is going to try to arrest me. You shouldn't let him get away with it. If I am arrested they'll lynch me, while if you kill Brady, you shall earn a reward." Author Robert M. Utley stated that there was a "plot to rid the country of William Brady and the Regulators laid plans" for his assassination. The Regulators would have known that Brady would be in town that morning for court.

In spite of the insight provided above, it is necessary to examine the notion of whether or not Billy the Kid and those accompanying him had, in fact, planned in advance to kill Brady or merely seized the opportunity when they spotted him coming down the street.

What we have here is a crime and a crime scene, and it needs to be investigated as such. If one or more persons are planning to kill someone, doing it in the middle of the town of Lincoln seems, on the surface, to be a bad idea. In spite of the inclement weather, hundreds of people are residing or doing business within only a few blocks of where the crime occurred.

According to Sederwall, the notion that the Regulators were merely hanging out in the corral doesn't carry much logic. As a result of the weather, the corral would have been muddy. Furthermore, it was a cold day. There were more comfortable and warmer places to hang out in Lincoln.

If the Regulators had made a trip to town with the intention to kill Brady, they would have been aware of better places to accomplish the nefarious deed. For example, the trip the sheriff made from his residence to Lincoln covered five miles of, for the most part, uninhabited countryside replete with places suitable for ambush. The Regulators could have hidden just off the trail and blown Brady out of the saddle and escaped without anyone hearing or seeing anything. That particular geography is known in cop parlance as a "kill zone," and would have been far more suitable for such an act than the middle of downtown Lincoln. There would have been no witnesses, thus no case. In addition, there would have been no one to return fire.

Indeed, a substantial argument can be made for the notion that Billy the Kid and the Regulators had arrived in town not to kill Sheriff Brady but to testify before the grand jury. Recall that shortly after witnessing Tunstall's murder and the attempt to cover up the crime, the Kid and his fellows did not enter into an immediate confrontation or conflict. Instead, they chose to travel to Lincoln and provide sworn statements to the justice of the peace and obtain legal warrants for the arrest of the sheriff and his appointed deputies, warrants that the governor subsequently and illegally declared void, an act that allowed the sheriff and his men to get away with murder. The notion of the Kid and his band traveling to Lincoln to testify at a formal jury is entirely consistent with previous behavior. Writer Maurice G. Fulton, in his book *History of the Lincoln County War*, stated that some of the Regulators, "expected in court either as witnesses or as the accused, had gathered in Lincoln during the evening of March 31 to be on hand for the court session."

The evidence shows that the Regulators rode through a storm to come to Lincoln not for the express purpose of killing Brady but to testify before the grand jury. If they had come to kill Brady, it would have been easier and more intelligent to do it as he rode up the valley from his house. As the Regulators sat huddled in the corral waiting for the storm to abate, it is likely that they were waiting for court to convene; they were waiting for one more try to force the legal system to work.

There is more. When Brady first arrived in town and traveled to the Wortley Hotel for breakfast, he would have ridden past the location where the Regulators were waiting out the storm. At that time he was alone. If the Regulators wanted him dead and didn't care who saw them, why did they not fire on the sheriff at that point?

It is a simple matter to speculate that sometime during breakfast, or while he was conducting business at the Murphy-Dolan Store, Brady was likely apprised of the presence of Billy the Kid and the Regulators in town. This would account for Brady gathering Mathews, Hindman, Long, and Peppin around him.

It is also possible, even likely, that by this time the Regulators learned that the court session would not take place as previously announced. As a result, they would not be allowed to testify. It is reasonable to believe that, in their minds, this was one more example of Sheriff Brady obstructing justice, that their last legal option for justice had been removed from them. At this point the possibility exists that they were convinced that there would be no justice from those sworn to deliver it, so they decided in the moment to dispense it themselves.

This pattern provides a strong argument for the prospect that the killing of Brady was not a planned, well-thought-out event. If it had been, the sheriff would have been gunned down between his house and town or during his first pass up the street. Instead, it seemed to be more of a crime of passion and/or spontaneity born of frustration, a spur-of-the-moment decision to achieve justice. It is quite likely that the Kid and his followers did not decide to kill Brady until nine a.m., April 1, 1878. Remember, the Regulators had been subjected to, and were victims of, a corrupt system inhabited by Lincoln businessmen and law enforcement officials up to and including the governor of the territory.

Sederwall hastens to point out that there is more to this killing that the historians and writers either missed or misrepresented. Every account of the Brady killing states that the sheriff and his four deputies "walked" down the main street of town when the shooting occurred. The first time this was described in this manner was in 1939 when writer Maurice G. Fulton recorded a description provided by Juan Peppin, son of Sheriff George Peppin, during an interview. The younger Peppin stated that Brady, his father, and the others were "walking down the street abreast." Fulton related this version in his subsequent writings. Researchers, historians, and others intent on producing their own volumes on Billy the Kid and the Lincoln County War simply copied Fulton's words and thought nothing more of it.

Sederwall determined that Brady and his men were not walking at all, that they were all on horseback when they were fired on by the Regulators. There are several points to support this contention.

First, the streets of Lincoln were deep with mud from the heavy rains of the previous several hours. There were no boardwalks or sidewalks as we know them today. If one walked down the main street in Lincoln in 1878, one walked *in* the street. It does not make sense, given that Brady and his men all possessed horses, that they would walk in the mud.

Second, horse professionals tell us that these animals have four natural gaits. From fast to slow, they are gallop or run, canter, trot, and walk. When horsemen use the term "walk," they are referring to a particular gait of the horse they are riding. Juan Peppin knew this, was intimate with this kind of language. Fulton, however, was not familiar with such terminology, nor apparently were any of the writers who followed him.

Third, Juan Peppin told Fulton that Brady and his men walked down the street "abreast." Men don't walk abreast; horses walk abreast. Fulton was unacquainted with such horse culture language and got it wrong.

Fourth, recall that Brady rode his horse to the Wortley Hotel, rode it from the hotel to the Murphy-Dolan Store, and tied it to the hitch rail there. It does not make sense that Brady would ride his horse across the muddy street from the Wortley Hotel to the Murphy-Dolan Store, then leave it at that rail and proceed on foot back through the same muck and mire he had traveled earlier on horseback.

Fifth, Brady was close to fifty years old and, from an examination of photographs, clearly overweight. According to the description of his body, he was wearing a heavy coat, carrying a heavy revolver, and toting a nine-pound Winchester rifle. He was also wearing spurs. It is unreasonable to believe that, given Brady's bulk, his armament, his coat, and his spurs, he would undertake to wade down a muddy, sloppy street, one that he had just ridden up on his horse.

Sixth, horses are flight animals. It is in their nature to run from danger. When startled, say by a gunshot, they will often rear up and lunge forward or wheel around to escape. As Brady and his men were walking their horses down the street, the animals would have been relatively calm, heads down, moving slowly, riders sitting their saddles easy. The moment the Regulators opened fire, the horses would have been startled and thrown their heads up. Next, their front feet would have come off the ground as they lunged forward in an attempt to move away from the gunfire.

When Brady was delivered the killing shot early in the firing—he was struck in the back and from the left—his body would have gone limp. With the horse lunging forward, the sheriff would have been thrown back over the saddle's cantle onto the horse's rump. His feet would have been in front of him with his body moving backward. As he slid off the horse's rump, the animal would have been running out from under him. Brady's feet would have been dragged out of the stirrups, and his body would fall to the ground, landing in a sitting position. Gorgonio Wilson, an eyewitness to the shooting, stated that he saw Brady "fall to a sitting position." Falling from the back of a startled horse to a sitting position on the ground has been experienced by many a horseman. Had Brady been afoot, his body would have fallen forward on being struck by the bullets.

There exists another piece of evidence suggestive of the notion that Brady and his posse were on horseback when the shooting occurred. The evidence encountered by Sederwall also provides for the possibility that, on fleeing, Billy the Kid may have climbed onto Sheriff Brady's horse and made his escape. According to Dr. Henry F. Hoyt in his book *A Frontier Doctor* (1929), Billy the Kid "stepped up to the counter in Howard and McMasters' store, picked up a piece of paper, and rapidly wrote for me a formal bill of sale, just as if it was a purchase, signed it and had it witnessed by the proprietors, probably the two best known men in the Panhandle at the time." The Howard and McMasters' Store was located in Tascosa, Texas.

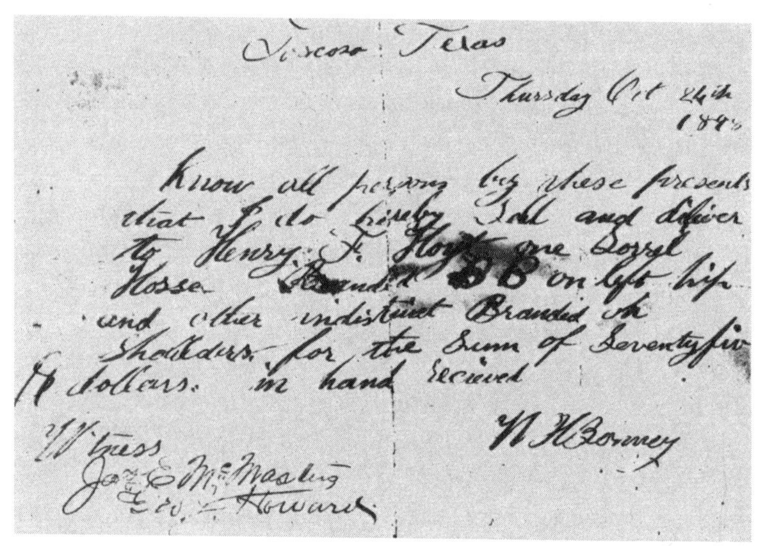

Tascosa Texas

Thursday Oct 24th
18[illegible]

Know all persons by these presents that I do hereby Sell and deliver to Henry F. Hoyt one Sorrel Horse Branded BB on left hip and other indistinct Brands on Shoulders for the Sum of Seventyfive $ dollars. in hand received

W H Bonney

Witness
Jas. E. McMasters
Geo. J. Howard

A bill of sale for Sheriff Brady's horse from Billy the Kid to Henry Hoyt
PANHANDLE PLAINS MUSEUM

The bill of sale refers to a "BB" brand on the left hip. Page 359 of the Lincoln County Brand Book shows that this brand was registered to William Brady. According to Dr. Hoyt, he had no knowledge that the horse had ever belonged to Brady until 1921. Hoyt sent a copy of the bill of sale to Charles A. Siringo, a former lawman who was writing a book about Billy the Kid. Siringo took the bill of sale to James Brady, William Brady's oldest son. James Brady's response on seeing the paper: "My God. It was my father's horse that he was riding when killed by the Kid!"

At the time of the sale, Dr. Hoyt asked the Kid where the horse came from. The Kid responded by saying, "There's a story connected with him." That story, the true one according to Steve Sederwall, has now been told.

Chapter Seven

THE SHOOTING AT BLAZER'S MILL

During the oft-related gunfight at Blazer's Mill, near Mescalero, New Mexico, two men were killed and one wounded, and the event served to further the growing reputation of the outlaw Billy the Kid. This episode was invariably handled by most who wrote about Billy the Kid and the Lincoln County War. The incident is presented here to further demonstrate the difference between the manner in which this event has long been treated and what is more likely the truth as discerned from an investigative analysis conducted by Steve Sederwall.

History tells us that on April 4, 1878, Billy the Kid and the Regulators stopped for a meal at Blazer's Mill, located on the upper Rio Tularosa in Lincoln County. The mill was owned by Dr. Joseph H. Blazer, who earned the term "doctor" as a result of being assigned to pull soldiers' teeth during the Civil War. Following the war Blazer came to New Mexico, where he served as one of the first commissioners of the newly founded Lincoln County.

The bearded, forty-eight-year-old Blazer owned a two-story house he leased to the federal government to use as headquarters for the Mescalero Apache Agency. Nearby stood a sawmill. The agency was operated by Maj. Frederick Godfroy. Godfroy sold food, blankets, and other provisions and supplies to the Murphy-Dolan Store at cut-rate prices. As it was later discovered, all of the items sold by Godfroy had been stolen from the government.

Godfroy's wife often cooked and sold meals to travelers, the food taken from the store of government provisions dedicated to the Indians on the reservation. Travelers were charged for the meals, and the money was pocketed by the Godfroys.

As the Regulators dined on the meal prepared by Mrs. Godfroy, a forty-five-year-old Texan named Andrew L. "Buckshot" Roberts rode up on a mule and leading a packhorse. Roberts had been a member of the posse that murdered Tunstall, and the Regulators held a warrant for his arrest. Frank Coe spotted Roberts and went outside to talk to him. Coe later related that the two sat on the porch and talked for half an hour as Coe "begged [Roberts] to surrender." Roberts refused. He was aware of the killings of Morton, Baker, Brady, and Hindman at the hands of the Regulators and did not care to be added to the growing list of victims.

Presently, Charlie Bowdre and John Middleton, and perhaps others, came out and confronted Roberts. A gunfight ensued, and the historical accounts tell us that George Coe had a finger shot off, Middleton was shot in the chest, and Bowdre shot Roberts in the stomach. Frank Coe was quoted as saying, "Bowdre shot him through, from one side to the other. The dust flew from his clothes from both sides." Wounded, Roberts retreated to a nearby empty room. Dick Brewer took up a position behind a woodpile from which he hoped to get a rifle shot at Roberts. The woodpile was located several dozen yards opposite the room in which Roberts had taken refuge. When Brewer peeked over the top of the woodpile, Roberts sent a bullet through his head, killing him instantly. The Regulators rode away, and Roberts died from his wound the following morning.

Most of the crime scene is gone today, with the exception of one nearly intact building and some scattered ruins. The building in which Buckshot Roberts took refuge burned down in 1884. Today, the only way to examine what happened there is through public records and the testimony of those who were present. During the 1930s, Lincoln County historian Maurice Garland Fulton corresponded with A. N. Blazer, who still lived at the mill. A. N. Blazer was present during the shooting in 1878 and was an eyewitness to the events. He was thirteen years old. A. N. Blazer wrote three letters to Fulton (April 10, 1930; April 24, 1931; and August 27, 1937) in which he recreated various aspects of the episode.

Blazer wrote that Buckshot Roberts arrived at the mill late in the evening, contradicting accounts put forth by various writers. Blazer stated that "five minutes could not have passed from the time Roberts dismounted from his mule and the firing of the first shot, which would give time for little, if any, conversation."

Blazer also reported that following the trial of Billy the Kid in Mesilla several years later, where the young outlaw was sentenced to hang, lawmen who were escorting him back to Lincoln stopped at the mill to spend the night. Blazer's sister, identified as "Mrs. Thompson," waited on the deputies and the Kid, who were fed breakfast the following morning. She listened closely as the Kid related what happened during the gunfight at the mill.

The Kid claimed that Buckshot Roberts shot Frank Coe and then turned and ran to take refuge in the nearby room. A short time later Roberts killed Brewer. During the brief gunfight the Kid counted six shots fired by Roberts from his rifle, the total number of rounds a Winchester carbine could carry in a magazine. The Kid later told Thompson that he knew a man like Roberts, as experienced with firearms as he was, would not carry a live round under the hammer. After Roberts fired off his six rounds, the Kid rushed his hiding place before he could reload. The door to the room in which Roberts took refuge was slightly open because Roberts had been firing through it at the Regulators from his position. When his rifle was empty, Roberts looked down to reload. The loading gate on the Winchester is on the right side; thus, to reload, Roberts would have held the rifle in his left hand as he prepared to feed fresh cartridges into it with his right. When he heard the Kid coming toward him, Roberts reached for the doorknob with his right hand to slam the door.

Billy the Kid fired through the partially closed door, the bullet entering Roberts's body, according to Blazer, "just above the hip bone on the left side and ranged a little up." This indicates that the Kid, on running toward the door, dropped and slid across the boardwalk, falling to a prone position and likely laying on the boards, his handgun pointing slightly upward and very close to the partially closed door. He fired a shot through the door, striking Roberts, and then jumped to his feet and left. Roberts then slammed the door shut.

Blazer further described Roberts, in pain as he lay on his deathbed, providing the same account as that related by Billy the Kid. The story is partly corroborated, according to Blazer, "by the bullet hole through the door facing, and the powder burn on the wood showed that the gun must have been fired while very near touching the surface."

According to a number of published accounts, both Buckshot Roberts and Dick Brewer were buried in a single grave nearby. An on-site examination of the gravesite conducted by Sederwall, however, revealed the existence of two separate markers and what are clearly two separate graves.

Chapter Eight

THE BURNING OF THE McSWEEN HOUSE

While Billy the Kid received virtually all of the major headlines touting him as the most notorious outlaw in the American Southwest, the truth is that he was no worse than many of those who opposed him. The principal difference was that the Kid owned little to nothing and barely got by with an occasional job and sometimes by rustling cattle. Unlike other famous outlaws, Billy the Kid never robbed banks or trains. By contrast, those who opposed him were men with money and/or power: J. J. Dolan of the Murphy-Dolan enterprises, the large ranchers, and the area law enforcement as well as the military establishment. This was never made clearer than in the incident involving the burning of Alexander McSween's house, which was accompanied by the killing of several men.

On July 14, 1878, a party of Regulators rode into Lincoln, each one armed and prepared for a fight. In his book *Frontier Fighter*, George Coe said that he and his companions "rode into Lincoln, fifty men strong without being reported. There was no moon." Coe was in error—there was a full moon that night. On close inspection it was discovered that much of what Coe wrote in his book and has been attributed to him was exaggerated or invented.

The Regulators still held warrants for some of the members of the posse that killed John H. Tunstall. It is also believed they were coming to Lincoln to provide some level of protection to the late

Tunstall's partner, Alexander McSween, a sworn enemy of Dolan and company.

On entering the town, the Regulators divided their force, seeking optimum fields of fire. Several took up positions at the Ellis Store; another group stationed themselves in the home of Jose Montaño. The remainder, including Billy the Kid, made their way to McSween's house, where they forted up.

Lincoln County sheriff George Peppin was out of town. He left a force under the direction of Deputy Jack Long. This force consisted of only a handful of men, but they occupied the Torreon, a two-story-tall stone tower constructed years earlier as a defense against raiding Apaches. Apparently apprised of the visit of the Regulators, the sheriff's force climbed into the tower before the Kid and his band arrived. Not a shot was fired by the lawmen as the Regulators rode past the tower.

McSween was the owner of the Torreon and the land it stood on, as well as the house next to it, wherein resided Saturnino Baca. McSween grew angry on learning that his property had been occupied by the sheriff's men, an act facilitated by tenant Baca. In lawyerly fashion McSween served notice on Baca, to wit: "Sir, I want you to vacate the property now occupied by you at once. Unless you leave the house within three days, proceedings will be instituted against you without further notice." Since Baca allowed the deputies to occupy the property, if Baca were removed, then the deputies could be regarded as trespassing. The landlord, McSween, had the legal right to evict trespassers.

Baca, an ex-sheriff and former officer with the New Mexico Volunteers during the Civil War, was incensed on reading McSween's eviction notice. He immediately sought help from his friend Lt. Col. Nathan A. M. Dudley, the post commander at nearby Fort Stanton. Dudley sent his post surgeon, Dr. Daniel Appel, to Lincoln to look into the goings-on. Appel spent his time running negotiation between McSween and the occupiers of the Torreon. He concluded that the situation was bad, tense.

Deputy Long knew that by controlling the Torreon he had a distinct advantage. Regulator Josiah G. "Doc" Scurlock sent Long a written promise that he and his deputies could leave the Torreon without fear of being fired upon. Long refused to vacate, so the Regulators dug in for a war.

Gun ports were cut into the houses occupied by the Regulators. Doors were reinforced, windows covered. Notches in which to rest rifles were cut into the parapets of the flat roofs. Around this time Sheriff Peppin returned to town. Peppin had been sheriff for only thirty days and, like those before him, was little more than a tool of the Murphy-Dolan cartel. Like all other sheriffs in New Mexico Territory, Peppin had been commissioned as a deputy United States marshal. He carried with him federal murder warrants for Frank and George Coe, Doc Scurlock, Charles Bowdre, Henry Brown, and Billy the Kid. Peppin also held a territorial warrant for McSween related to an attempted murder charge.

Peppin ordered Deputy Long to go to the McSween house and arrest those for whom he held warrants. As he approached the house, he was fired on. Long scurried for cover, and the shooting got under way, a "war" that was to last for five days. Perceiving a need for reinforcements, Peppin sent a rider to a location near San Patricio to retrieve a posse that had been working there. As the shooting raged, Lincoln residents snuck out of town at every opportunity.

Having no success at negotiating a peace, Dr. Appel decided to leave Lincoln and return to Fort Sumner. Along the road he encountered John Kinney and his band of outlaws, who referred to themselves as the Seven Rivers Warriors. Riding with them was Jessie Evans. Kinney and his men had been busy making raids throughout the county stealing livestock. When Appel explained what was going on in Lincoln, Kinney led his men on a charge through town and fired their weapons at the McSween house. The back-and-forth shooting continued until dark.

The following day sporadic gunfire could be heard throughout the town. When Peppin's San Patricio posse arrived, he stationed them in nearby hills immediately south of town to take shots at McSween's snipers. Only a horse and mule were hit. As it began to dawn on Peppin that his efforts were useless, he drafted a message to Lieutenant Colonel Dudley: "If it is in your power to loan me one of your Howitzers, you would confer a great favor on the majority of the people in this County, who are being persecuted by a lawless mob."

Peppin was not aware that Dudley was legally prohibited from entering the fray. Four days after Peppin took office, the United States Congress passed the Posse Comitatus Act, June 18, 1878, which prevented the army from "executing the laws" unless "expressly authorized by the Constitution or by act of Congress." If Dudley ordered his troops into Lincoln, he could face discharge, a fine of ten thousand dollars, and two years in jail. He sent a note expressing his willingness to help and said that his "sympathies . . . are most earnestly and sincerely with you on the side of the law."

Dudley was aware of the law and was receptive to a loophole that could get his forces into the fight. J. J. Dolan provided one. He, along with John Kinney, wrote a note to Dudley and had the puppet Sheriff Peppin sign it. "Am very sorry I can't get the assistance I asked for but I will do the best I can. The McSween party fired on your soldier when coming into town. My men on seeing him tried their best to cover him, but of no use. The soldier will explain the circumstances to you." Dolan and Kinney lied, and Peppin went along with it, providing Dudley the excuse he needed. Dudley seized the moment and began making plans to enter Lincoln with a force.

During the gunfight Fernando Herrera, a Regulator, shot Charles "Lallycooler" Crawford, making him the first casualty of the battle. Crawford was a posse member occupying a spot on the hill south of town. Crawford was bleeding badly, crying out in agony. Peppin and his men were too frightened to go assist him. Dr. Appel, who had returned to Lincoln, risked his own life in racing to the downed man and offering aid. Crawford was taken by wagon to Fort Stanton, where he died on July 24.

On the night of July 18, Ben Ellis went out to the corral behind his store to feed his horse. He was illuminated by a nearly full moon. One of Peppin's men spotted him and fired two shots. The second shot struck Ellis in the neck, dropping him. He managed to crawl back to his house.

Dr. Ealy and his family lived in a house at the back of the Tunstall Store. They barricaded the windows with trunks and furniture and lay on the floor, praying that stray bullets would not strike their children. When they ran out of water, Mrs. Ealy and Sue Gates left the house carrying several buckets down to the Rio Bonito. No one fired on the women.

That evening two men came to the back door of the house. They had waded the river and come up behind the houses and buildings in order to keep from being seen by the lawmen in the Torreon. To get to Ealy's back door without being spotted, they were forced to crawl through the mud and manure of Tunstall's corral. They begged the doctor to come and give aid to the wounded Ellis. Ealy agreed to accompany the men back through the mud to the river. As they approached the Ellis Store, however, they were fired on and were forced to return without seeing Ellis.

The next morning Ealy was determined to go to Ellis. He gathered up his baby, and amid the tearful pleas of his wife, left the house and walked down the middle of the street toward the Ellis house. Not a shot was fired. Ealy was able to dress Ellis's wound, and the storekeeper survived.

On the morning of July 19, Lieutenant Colonel Dudley led a column of forty troopers into Lincoln. Every officer from Fort Stanton save one rode with Dudley. Dudley came ready to wage war: He brought a Gatling gun, a howitzer, a wagonload of ammunition, and rations for three days.

Dudley later testified at a subsequent court of inquiry that he led his soldiers into Lincoln only to protect the women and children. The truth is, such was not his goal but his excuse. Dudley, like James J. Dolan, had lied. It was subsequently learned that on July 18 Dolan had ridden to Fort Stanton to meet with Dudley to hatch a plan allowing the officer to skirt the Posse Comitatus Act and involve the US military in the fight. Both men lied under oath.

The discussion between Dolan and Dudley was overheard by Alexander Rubber, who was at the fort at the time. Rubber testified that the two men talked about how the army intervening in the conflict would sway the fight in Dolan's favor. When Dudley learned that Rubber had heard the plans to involve the military in the fight, he had him confined to the fort. Rubber had violated no law, and since he was a private citizen, Dudley had no authority over him whatsoever. Rubber stated that Dudley threatened to lock him in the post jail, perhaps even hang him, but then promised to let him leave the fort in "four or five days" after the affair in Lincoln was settled.

James A. Tomlinson, who would later become a probate judge, took the stand during Dudley's inquiry. Tomlinson testified that he was at the fort in a sleeping room during the time of the fight in Lincoln. He was awakened by the sound of men talking in the hallway. One of the men, said Tomlinson, was John Kinney, the other unknown to him. Tomlinson testified that the unknown man had said that "as far as he was concerned, and others, they were getting tired of the Lincoln County fight, and he and the others had come for the purpose of making a noise, and they thought there was no use in waiting any longer, as they could do nothing without the assistance of the military. Kinney's reply was 'assistance would be had.'"

Tomlinson further testified that the unknown man talked about killing McSween supporters who happened to be at the fort. Kinney then said, "No, that would not do, that they must make a killing down there. Other parties could be, or would be, attended to afterwards."

The court recorded that Dolan and Dudley had entered into a conspiracy, stating that, "A conspiracy is defined to be an agreement between two or more to do an unlawful act, or to do an unlawful act by unlawful means."

A number of other witnesses testified that Dolan and Dudley had discussed the prospect of sending troops to the fight. When Dolan testified, he lied and said he "never had any conversation with Colonel Dudley in the hall mentioned in that building. I had conversation with Colonel Dudley in Lieutenant Goodwin's quarters but nothing in relation to Lincoln County affairs." Dolan would have had the court believe that during the middle of the biggest gun battle during the Lincoln County War he decided to take a leisurely ride to Fort Stanton and chat with Dudley about topics other than the fight. For Dolan's testimony to be true, everyone else in court, including the court recorder, had to have been lying.

It should be pointed out here that while Dolan and Dudley were conversing, Dolan was under indictment and had an outstanding warrant for his arrest as an accessory to murder. Dolan's partner, John Riley, was also under indictment and had an outstanding warrant for cattle theft. Dudley was aware of this, yet he carried on and plotted with wanted men as if it were not important.

When Dudley testified, he stated that he had no intention of going to war with McSween, in spite of the fact that he ordered to Lincoln forty mounted, armed, and provisioned troopers; a cannon; a Gatling gun; ammunition; and rations.

In the end it became clear that both Dolan and Dudley were lying under oath and that the testimony pointed to a conspiracy between the two men to violate the law. It was further determined that no one had fired upon any of Dudley's soldiers, that the act was concocted in order to initiate the military's involvement.

Despite Dudley's insistence that he led troops into Lincoln solely for the purpose of protecting women and children, two points were brought out in court. (1) He set up a cannon and ordered it pointed to the Montaño house, in which resided Mrs. Montaño and her children, including two girls. According to Mrs. Montaño's testimony, Dudley pointed the cannon not only at her house but also at the room she and her daughters occupied. (2) Mrs. Montaño ran from her house to Dudley and begged him for protection. Mrs. Montaño testified that, in responding, Dudley "said he had not soldiers sufficient, not even in the fort, and for that reason he could not give me protection."

Not only had Dudley lied about coming to Lincoln to protect women and children, he actually *refused* them protection.

Dudley then ordered his men to surround the McSween house. When McSween became aware of this maneuver, he scribbled a note to Dudley and gave it to his ten-year-old niece for delivery. The note read:

Gen'l Dudley, USA

Would you have the kindness to let me know why soldiers surround my house?

Before blowing up my property I would like to know the reason. The Constable is here and has warrants for the arrest of Sheriff Peppin and posse for murder and larceny.

Respectfully,

A. A. McSween

Dudley directed Lieutenant Goodwin to reply to McSween's note:

> *I am directed by the commanding officer to inform you that no soldiers have surrounded your house and that he desires to hold no correspondence with you; if you desire to blow up your house, the commanding officer does not object, provided it does not injure any United States soldiers.*

Note how Dudley twisted McSween's words to make it seem as if the lawyer implied that he would blow up his own house, and placed such an act in the form of a threat to the troopers. Dudley was trying his best to manipulate the brief correspondence with McSween in his favor. Either that or he was incredibly stupid.

When Billy the Kid took the stand during Dudley's court of inquiry, he stated, "Three soldiers came and stood in front of the house, in front of the windows. Mr. McSween wrote a note to the officer in charge asking what the soldiers were placed there for."

Dudley was playing a dangerous game and was attempting to initiate a fight. He placed soldiers in front of the windows of the McSween house solely in an attempt to draw fire. Had this occurred, he would have had all the excuse he needed to turn the cannon onto the house and blow it apart, killing everyone within. We know this to be true because according to McSween's wife, Susan, Dudley told her that "if a shot was fired from our house at the soldiers, or near them, that he would turn the canon loose."

Dudley's troops managed to run McSween's men from the Montaño and Ellis houses, leaving the only stronghold for the Regulators at the McSween house. It was clear that if any attempted to leave the house they would be cut down. This seemed to be how Dudley wanted to end the confrontation.

Susan McSween managed to sneak out of the house. She crawled on the ground until she was some distance from the dwelling, at which point she rose and marched into Dudley's camp. The first person she encountered was Sheriff Peppin. She tried to reason with him, but Peppin told her that if she did not want her house burned down she needed to see that the men inside came out. Peppin told her that he would have them today, "dead or alive."

Mrs. McSween brushed past Peppin and sought out Dudley. The two entered into a heated argument, and Dudley informed her of her husband's plan to blow up his own house. Mrs. McSween explained that such a thing was nonsense. Dudley offered to show her the letter. When Mrs. McSween reached for the letter, Dudley turned to Sgt. Thomas S. Baker, who was standing nearby. According to Baker's testimony, Dudley ordered him to shoot Mrs. McSween "if she attempted to take the letter out of his hand." Baker stated that Dudley smiled as he gave the order. Remember, Dudley was the man who stated that he came to Lincoln to protect the women and children, yet he threatened to have a woman shot for wanting to read a letter.

Mrs. McSween returned to her house. By the time she arrived, Dudley had ordered the cannon aimed at the front door. Troopers continued to stand in front of the windows daring the McSween men to shoot. Around one p.m. Sheriff Peppin ordered his posse to set fire to the house.

Andy Boyle was a member of Peppin's posse. Like several others in the posse, Boyle was not from Lincoln County; he was a cattle rustler from Texas who arrived for the fight. Boyle set the fire at the "back door of the kitchen on the northwest corner . . . with a sack of shavings and chips" and some timber he found in the stable.

As the fire raged and expanded, consuming the house, soldiers remained standing outside the windows. Peppin and Dudley waited, knowing that the flames would soon drive the Regulators out into the open where they would be easy to shoot down. By nine p.m. Mrs. McSween left the house and the fire had pushed the men into one room.

Suddenly five men decided to make a break and dashed out the back door. One of them, Harvey Morris, was gunned down. Billy the Kid testified that he then ran out the back door with a second group of Regulators—Jose Chavez, Vicente Romero, and Francisco Zamora—along with Alexander McSween. The Kid said they had to jump over the body of Harvey Morris, then ran "towards the Tunstall Store and then turned towards the river." McSween was shot down and died with five bullets in him.

Another wave of escapees included Tom Folliard and Yginio Salazar. Salazar fell to the ground with three bullet wounds. Forty-eight years later Salazar related that he had been struck in one hand, his left shoulder, and his left side. He stated:

> *I lay unconscious for a while. When I regained consciousness the fight was over. The Murphy men were laughing, singing, and drinking whiskey. I thought the only way I stood a chance to live was to play dead. I sprawled as motionless as possible.*
>
> *Andy Boyle kicked me to see if I was dead. The heavy boots struck my wounded side and the torture was so terrible that I could hardly stand it. Then I felt the muzzle of his rifle pressed against my heart and knew that my time had come. Then I heard old man [Milo Pierce] tell Boyle not to waste a bullet on me as I was already dead.*

Salazar feigned death for three hours before he was able to crawl away and seek help.

The following morning there was only a pile of ashes where once stood the McSween house. Alexander McSween was interred in the tiny cemetery behind the store he operated with his friend and partner John Tunstall. Tunstall lay in a similar grave beside him.

Billy the Kid and his companions escaped into the night. It is easy to imagine the disappointment felt by this band of men. They had ridden into town to serve legal warrants and to offer protection to their friend, Alexander McSween. Their quest for justice was thwarted by the very forces that should have stood for law and order—the office of the Lincoln County sheriff and the United States military. Surely the notion of cooperating with agents of authority in the future appeared as a dim prospect.

A number of publications dealing with Billy the Kid and the Lincoln County War portray Sheriff Peppin and his deputies, as well as Colonel Dudley and his soldiers, as attempting to restore law and order in the town of Lincoln. Following Sederwall's in-depth analysis of the "war," he concluded that more violations of the law were committed by the men responsible for law enforcement than by those who were identified as outlaws.

Chapter Nine

COUNTERFEIT MONEY

A criminal activity that reared its ugly head around the time of the Lincoln County War was related to counterfeit money, specifically the passing of counterfeit bills in a variety of transactions. This activity involved a significant number of Lincoln County residents, among them outlaw Billy Wilson, White Oaks rancher W. W. West, James J. Dolan, and Billy the Kid.

For reasons not understood, according to Steve Sederwall, every writer who treated the Lincoln County War and the outlaw Billy the Kid either completely ignored or provided all too brief attention to the issue of counterfeit money. This seems odd, observes Sederwall, for it was this very activity that brought federal investigators into the region.

According to Sheriff Pat Garrett, Billy the Kid and his gang stole cattle from John H. Chisum's ranch at the Bosque Grande, located twenty-eight miles north of Roswell, New Mexico. Garrett stated that Chisum owed the Kid and his associates "$600 each for services rendered during the [Lincoln County] war." Chisum never paid, and the Kid and his gang took the cattle in "trade." During October 1879 the cattle were driven to Frank Yerby's ranch, rebranded, and turned loose on the range. Later the cattle were sold to a group of "Colorado beef buyers, [with Billy the Kid] telling them they were employed in settling up Chisum's business."

For reasons unknown, none of the numerous researchers into Lincoln County history questioned this odd arrangement. The Kid's story about working for Chisum might have been believable had the cattle worn Chisum's brand, but the outlaw had them rebranded. This incident piqued the interest of Sederwall, and he set about to investigate.

The actions of the beef buyers were also confusing. They purchased 118 head of cattle from a man who stated that he was working for John Chisum, taking him entirely at his word. Later Chisum rode up to Colorado and retrieved his cattle that the buyers had paid for, and they did nothing to stop him. In a normal situation the buyers would have fought to keep the cattle they purchased, received reimbursement, or sent for the law. They did none of that. What legitimately run operation would not fight to maintain their investment? This strange encounter is a perfect example of, in police parlance, a "tell."

The appearance of the Colorado beef buyers on the Lincoln County scene occurred at the same time counterfeit money began to circulate in the area. This was no coincidence. Any historian worth his or her salt would look for a connection. If the beef buyers were paying for the cattle with counterfeit money, they would be unlikely to raise a big fuss or go running to the law when Chisum took his herd back. As any cop will inform you: In order to establish a connection, follow the money.

Sederwall's investigation led along a winding and convoluted trail that stretched from Lincoln to New York City, San Francisco, Missouri, Texas, and elsewhere. For more than one hundred years, no one had penetrated the mystery of the origin of the counterfeit money passed in Lincoln County, New Mexico, money passed by Billy the Kid, among others. This is coupled with another mystery, and that has to do with the appearance on the scene of another iconic outlaw—Jesse James. Though the notion of outlaws Billy the Kid and Jesse James meeting up has arisen many times in the past, the prospect has been repeatedly shot down by some historians who claimed that these two men never encountered one another. The historians were wrong.

In his book *A Frontier Doctor*, Henry Hoyt describes his time in Las Vegas, New Mexico. He wrote that on Sundays he liked to dine at the Hot Springs Hotel, located six miles out of town. Hoyt stated that he "rode out one Sunday and found at the corner table the only vacant seat in the room. Glancing at the three guests already there, I was simply amazed to recognize the one on my left as Billy the Kid, urbane and smiling as ever. We shook hands, but neither mentioned a name." Hoyt sat himself at the table. One of the other men had finished his meal and excused himself.

Presently, the Kid turned to Dr. Hoyt and, referring to one of the other men at the table, said, "Hoyt, meet my friend Mr. Howard from Tennessee." The meal passed pleasantly. Following dinner Hoyt found himself alone with Billy the Kid. The Kid told Hoyt that Mr. Howard was, in fact, Jesse James. Jesse James lived in Nashville, Tennessee, from November 1875 to May 1881.

Miguel Otero, who would later become governor of New Mexico, also frequented the Hot Springs Hotel around this time. Winfred Scott Moore, a friend of Otero's, also happened to be an acquaintance of Jesse James. Moore told Otero that Mr. Howard was the famous outlaw.

There's more. The December 8, 1879, issue of the *Las Vegas Optic* featured the following comment: "Jesse James of Missouri was a guest at the Las Vegas Hot Springs from July 26 to July 29, 1979." Dr. Hoyt met James, aka Howard, on July 27.

What does all of this have to do with counterfeit money in Lincoln County? It is worthwhile to examine some connections established by Sederwall. The June 24, 1880, *Sacramento Daily Record-Union* ran an article reporting that "William Ralston and three others were arrested . . . on a charge of counterfeiting." Ralston was a brother-in-law of Frank James, Jesse's brother.

On July 8, 1881, Secret Service operative P. S. Tyrrell of the St. Louis office was informed that "Frank James has a large amount of counterfeit coin." Later Tyrrell observed James selling the counterfeit coins to the informer.

It is also interesting to note that during a time when Frank James was hiding out from the law, he moved to the small town of Nevada in Vernon County, Missouri. During this time a significant percentage of the population of Vernon County was made up of ex-Confederate soldiers. It turned out to be an ideal location for holding stolen cattle bought with counterfeit money, a reason why John W. Hays, a known counterfeiter, as well as Frank James, located there. During the Civil War both John Hays and Frank James rode with the guerilla leader William Clarke Quantrill.

During the summer of 1880, a number of counterfeit banknotes showed up in Sherman, Texas. Secret Service agent Azariah Wild traveled to Sherman and learned that a man named James Murphy Kirby from New York had arrived in town earlier to meet with one Walter Graham. An arrangement was made whereby Kirby would supply money to purchase cattle and resell them for a percentage of the profits. During his investigations Wild learned that Kirby was an alias for James Doyle, who was linked with New York counterfeiters.

Wild learned that the money used to purchase the cattle was counterfeit and produced in New York. Kirby/Doyle was shipping Graham packages of counterfeit bank notes from Chicago. The purchased cattle were to be herded into Missouri and placed on a ranch in Vernon County owned by John W. Hays. At this point Wild realized that the counterfeiting enterprise he was investigating was not limited to Texas and New Mexico, but rather turned out to be a widespread activity ranging from New York across the country into the American Southwest.

In 1879, a short time after the meeting between Billy the Kid and Jesse James in Las Vegas, the Kid and Tom Folliard rode to the ranch of Jim Cook located near the South Llano River in the Texas Hill Country. The Kid told old friend Cook that John Chisum owed him and Folliard money and explained how they planned to collect. According to Cook, "Billy said he and Tom would go back on the Pecos and round up thirty-two hundred of Uncle Johnny's steers. He would give me a bill of sale for them; I was to drive them to Kansas and sell them, pay myself, and bring him and Tom what was left." The Kid specifically told Cook to sell the cattle in Honeywell, Kansas; take the money to Kansas City and deposit it; wait for three days; and then return to the bank and withdraw it. Cook did as he was instructed, and several weeks later turned over nine thousand dollars to Billy the Kid.

To an investigator, that is another tell. Cook rode an unnecessarily long distance out of his way to deposit the money in Kansas City, waited for three days, and withdrew it. There was no logic in any of this unless the only objective was to have the money laundered. Cook deposited counterfeit money and a few days later withdrew good money.

Later the US Secret Service pieced together the details of this criminal enterprise. The Secret Service found John Hays, Doyle, and Foster "at Deer Trail, Colorado, when the gang were operating in the counterfeit hundreds." Why Colorado? John Hays's father-in-law owned a cattle ranch in Deer Trail. Nate Foster lived in Colorado. They were the "Colorado beef buyers." Buying and selling cattle was yet another way of laundering counterfeit money.

On June 8, 1880, the Missouri part of the counterfeit operation began to unravel when the Vernon County bank in the town of Nevada detected a counterfeit bill. The bill was passed by John Hays. Bank cashier J. W. Cockling confronted Hays, who eventually admitted he received the counterfeit bill from the Mastin Bank in Kansas City. It was the same bank where Jim Cook deposited the money he received from the sale of John Chisum's cattle that had been stolen by Billy the Kid.

Research by historian Ralph Peter Ganis revealed the fact that two brothers named Mastin started the bank with money from the Confederacy and that it catered to the beef industry.

The Mastins were Confederate sympathizers. Even as late as the 1880s, the Mastins and others like them were attempting to collapse the Union's financial system. Saturating the federal government's operation with bogus money was one way to accomplish that. Cook and Hays were laundering money at the Mastin Bank in Kansas City.

Because of the sluggish nature of communications and other factors during that time, eight months passed before the Secret Service accommodated the information relating to the counterfeiting operations. Acting on a lead, the Secret Service learned that a bundle of 104 counterfeit hundred-dollar banknotes were found in a haystack on the farm of John Hays in February 1881. Two days later eight more counterfeit bills were found in another of Hays's haystacks.

Agent Wallace Hall learned from Nevada County residents that Hays had been shipping cattle from the west into Missouri. He also learned that Hays traveled to Kansas City on a number of occasions to deposit large sums of money in the Mastin Bank. It was determined that this was counterfeit money and the intention was to have it laundered at the bank. Hall received information that the counterfeiting suspects were in Deer Trail, Colorado.

Hays learned that the Secret Service was on his trail. With Doyle and Foster he fled to White Oaks, New Mexico. On February 23, 1881, Hays signed a quitclaim deed transferring ownership of his Missouri farm to A. Kahn. The deed was notarized by Frank Lea at the Lincoln County Courthouse. Frank Lea's brother, Joseph, lived in Roswell, New Mexico. He, along with Jesse and Frank James, rode with Quantrill. Frank Lea was also a good friend of Pat Garrett.

On January 2, 1881, Agent Azariah Wild filed his daily report stating, "Information on the arrest of William Wilson, William Antrim alias Billy the Kid, with several members of their gang by Deputy U. S. Marshal Patrick F. Garrett has reached me." Three paragraphs later Wild recorded, "There is no trouble in arresting

Jesse James if he is not already arrested. I have put several men on his track who have been assisting me and would have arrested or caused his arrest when in New Mexico had I known he was wanted for any crime against the U. S. Government."

Note that Billy the Kid and Jesse James appeared in the same report. Bear in mind that Wild's responsibility here was to investigate counterfeiting. Billy the Kid and Jesse James both were clearly implicated in the counterfeiting operation.

On March 30, 1881, *the United States of America v. William Wilson* was the first case called before federal judge Warren H. Bristol. It was charged that Wilson "uttered and passed" counterfeit US money. He was also charged with robbing the US mail. Wilson was a close associate of Billy the Kid and a member of the Regulators.

According to the federal files, Wilson was known to have passed at least two hundred-dollar counterfeit bills, both drawn on the Merchants National Bank of New Bedford, Massachusetts. From 1863 to 1935, Congress authorized banks to issue banknotes bearing the bank's name.

Normally, when the law seized counterfeit money, plates, and press, such evidence was held until the case was adjudicated. After deposal of the case, all of the evidence, including the counterfeit money, was destroyed. There was one exception: The Secret Service maintains a collection of counterfeit coins and bills dating back to the birth of the Republic. The trail of the counterfeit money passed in New Mexico thus leads to the files of the Secret Service in Washington, DC.

In January 2010, Sederwall placed a call to the Secret Service public affairs officer Michael Sampson. This call led to the discovery in the Secret Service archives of one of the banknotes passed by Billy Wilson. A close examination of the bill by the

Secret Service yielded the information that it had been the work of ace counterfeiter William E. Brockway. Brockway, well known to the police in New York City, had been producing counterfeit bills since 1850. The discovery of Brockway's involvement subsequently led investigators on a long and snaking trail of manufacturing and passing counterfeit bills, many of which ended up in Lincoln County.

From Brockway's expert and precise counterfeiting work, the bills were marked as being issued from a variety of banks

William E. Brockway, professional counterfeiter
PHOTO COURTESY OF UNITED STATES SECRET SERVICE FILES

in Massachusetts, Pennsylvania, and Maryland. As a result of a widespread and effective criminal enterprise, the bills diffused throughout New York and Chicago; thence to Texas, Missouri, and Colorado; and eventually made their way to Lincoln County. Some of this counterfeit money wound up financing ranches.

On August 8, 1880, Chicago resident Miss N. M. Ferguson wrote a letter to US Secret Service Chicago Division chief Wallace W. Hall informing him that counterfeit banknotes were being passed in New Mexico. In her letter Ferguson enclosed a note from Fort Stanton, New Mexico, resident J. C. Delaney. With Delaney's note was a counterfeit bill that had been passed to him.

As it turned out, a short time before Ferguson's letter was received by the Secret Service, Frank Wallace, a Lincoln County resident and Secret Service informer, told agents that stolen cattle were being purchased in New Mexico Territory with counterfeit money. Hall was growing interested.

On August 24, 1880, Chief Hall wrote to a bureau chief named Brooks, telling him that "the Delaney letter, if true, in its statement gives some light as to who are operating in the counterfeit hundreds in that region." Hall learned from Ferguson the name of the suspect who had passed the counterfeit bill to Delaney: businessman James J. Dolan of Lincoln.

Chief Brooks sent Secret Service operative Azariah Wild to New Mexico Territory to investigate the passing of counterfeit money. Before Wild boarded the train to take him west, the Secret Service had identified the counterfeiters, where they lived, how and where they operated, how the money was being laundered, and how it was reaching the territory. Before Billy the Kid accepted the payment for the stolen cattle, the Secret Service was building a case against the counterfeiters.

The Secret Service learned that four men living in Colorado—James and Frank Doyle, John Hays, and Nate Foster—were buying cattle with counterfeit money. They were the Colorado beef

A counterfeit hundred-dollar bill passed in Lincoln County, New Mexico, during the 1880s
STEVE SEDERWALL COLLECTION

buyers mentioned by Pat Garrett who paid for cattle delivered to them by Billy the Kid.

In White Oaks, Nate Foster bought a saloon. A man going by the name W. H. West purchased a stable. Both men paid with counterfeit money. According to the Secret Service, West was an alias used by William H. Budd. West bought the stable from the Kid's friend Billy Wilson. The 1880 census shows West living in White Oaks with Samuel Dedrick. Dedrick was also paying for cattle using counterfeit bills that he obtained from West.

On October 2, 1880, Azariah Wild walked into LaRue's Store, located in the building that formerly housed the Tunstall Store. Wild was looking for James J. Dolan and found him. Dolan handed over a counterfeit hundred-dollar bill and told Wild that it had been passed to him by Billy Wilson. Following a search on October 4, Wild discovered several more counterfeit bills in Dolan's safe. Dolan explained that Wilson gave him the money for safekeeping and that he would come for it later.

According to Sederwall, there is a significant problem with Dolan's explanation. Dolan and Billy Wilson were bitter enemies. It makes no sense that Wilson would hand Dolan his money for safekeeping. Dolan was lying. He was in possession of counterfeit money but did not want to take the fall. He made up a story on the spot, making Wilson the fall guy. Dolan was known to be an accomplished crook.

On October 6, Ira Leonard, attorney for Billy the Kid, approached Agent Wild with a proposal. The Kid wanted to cut a deal, to become a government informant. Leonard told Wild that the Kid would give up the counterfeiters and testify against them if Governor Lew Wallace would make good on his promise to pardon him and if the United States attorney would drop the federal charges. In truth, all the Kid knew about the counterfeit ring involved Doyle and Hayes, the Colorado beef buyers. Neither the Kid nor Leonard was aware that the Secret Service already knew all they needed regarding Doyle and Hays.

On October 9, 1880, Wild wrote to Chief Brooks stating that James DeVours, the manager of the Carrizo Ranch west of White Oaks, would give up evidence on the counterfeiters for one thousand dollars. A meeting was arranged, related Wild, but before it could take place, DeVours disappeared. In a daily report to Brooks on October 28, Wild related that his identity seemed to be known by the counterfeiters and "there is no one I can get to assist me here that I can trust as every one (with one or two exceptions) who resides here, and who would otherwise assist me is scared that he will be killed."

There was good reason for real and potential informers to fear death at the hands of the counterfeiters. The May 21, 1880, *Santa Fe New Mexican* reported: "The information that enabled the Government officers to fix the handling of counterfeit money upon the Kid's gang came from a freighter named Smith. Soon afterward, while Smith was on his way from Las Vegas to Fort Sumner with a load of freight, he was waylaid and murdered by some of the gang."

Around this time Wild became aware that Billy the Kid or one or more of his associates, most likely Billy Wilson, was stopping the mail coach and reading his reports, thus providing the outlaw an advantage over the federal government. After opening and reading the mail, he sent it on. Wild informed Chief Brooks of his suspicions. Billy Wilson was later charged with robbing the US mail, an activity that did not commence until Wild came to Lincoln. All of this further suggested that the mail carrier himself was involved in the tampering. Wild tells Brooks that the "leading man of this gang [of counterfeiters] is W. H. West."

Lincoln County resident Paco Anaya stated that "Billy and his pals always had a lot of money," and that the Kid always paid, "no matter how much they asked for it, for a good horse, or for a good pistol, or for a good saddle, or for a good rifle. And this he did with cash money, but this was spurious money."

Anaya's statement is easy to understand when one realizes that the Kid, along with several others, was spending counterfeit money.

The subject of counterfeit money in 1880s New Mexico, in particular as it related to Billy the Kid, has long been overlooked or neglected by historians. The role it played was, in fact, prominent, involving not only the Kid and some of his cohorts but his most famous tracker—Pat Garrett. Counterfeit money also figured notably in events to come.

Despite the fact that he was no more of a criminal than a number of prominent Lincoln County businessmen, area ranchers, local lawmen, politicians, and even military officers at Fort Stanton,

Billy the Kid became the face of outlawry in southern New Mexico and the surrounding region. This was, in large part, because of the attention given to him, his gang, and related rustling and other activities by the newspapers. The Kid was good news copy and provided compelling headlines, and the media took advantage of this. Further, because so many of the establishment ranchers and businessmen suffered losses from the Kid's activities, they assisted in elevating him to the status of being the principal cause of trouble in Lincoln County and elsewhere. It didn't hurt that the young outlaw's popularity, according to some reports, was enhanced by his boyish charm and charismatic personality. It can be argued that such promotion of Billy the Kid as outlaw helped distract citizens from the criminal activities of those doing the promoting.

The principal difference between the crimes committed by Billy the Kid and those attributed to the members of the establishment and representatives of power is related to status. Billy the Kid's crimes can be classified as the blue-collar variety: cattle and horse rustling for the most part, supplemented here and there with possible mail tampering, with a handful of revenge and justice-related murders thrown in. The criminal offenses committed by those in power were more oriented to manipulation, cheating, intimidation, and bribery—so-called white-collar crimes.

As a result of his criminal activities, Billy the Kid, along with his gang, remained on the run. In pursuit of the outlaws was a posse headed by the lawman Pat Garrett. Though often referred to as sheriff, Garrett at this time was only the sheriff-elect. The reigning sheriff had been judged as being much too timid and inept to bring in the Kid, so the job was handed over to Garrett, who was commissioned as a special Lincoln County deputy. Garrett also carried a deputy United States marshal's commission signed by US Marshal John Sherman Jr.

There exists an interesting historical sidelight to Garrett's deputy US marshal commission: It was never official. US Marshal Sherman never commissioned Garrett. Sherman commissioned a man named John Hurley. Secret Service operative Azariah Wild contacted Sherman and asked him to appoint Garrett as a US deputy marshal. Sherman erroneously sent a second commission for Hurley. Wild, on his own, marked out Hurley's name on the form and replaced it with Garrett's. The presumptuous Wild determined unilaterally that Sherman had made a mistake. Technically, according to Sederwall, Garrett's subsequent role as the leader of the posse in pursuit of Billy the Kid and his gang was illegal.

Nevertheless, Garrett held two warrants for Billy the Kid: One was for the murder of Sheriff William Brady and the other for the murder of Andrew "Buckshot" Roberts. Both warrants were signed by Judge Bristol. Garrett's posse consisted of Jim East, Lee Hall, and Lon Chambers, all from the LX Ranch. Charlie Goodnight, who owned the LX Ranch, sent along his men to retrieve stolen cattle he believed to be in the possession of Billy the Kid. To this mix were added two of Goodnight's friends—Barney Mason and Frank Stewart. This group was accompanied by "Poker Tom" Emory, Louis "The Animal" Bousman, and Bob "Tenderfoot" Williams from the LIT Ranch. The posse headed out toward Fort Sumner in freezing cold and blowing snow. Some published accounts provide different numbers for this posse as well as identifying different participants.

The Kid, incidentally, had been referred to in print for the first time as "Billy the Kid" by the *Las Vegas Gazette* only fourteen days earlier. The name would stick with him for all time.

Garrett received information that the Kid, along with Billy Wilson, Dave Rudabaugh, Tom Folliard, Charlie Bowdre, and Tom Pickett, were at the Wilcox Ranch twelve miles east of Fort Sumner. The information included the notion that the gang was trying to sell a wagonload of beef. Garrett counted on the Kid and his gang returning to Fort Sumner, specifically to the old post hospital wherein resided Charlie Bowdre's wife and mother-in-law. Garrett stationed his men around the building. They spent their time sleeping and playing poker.

Around eight p.m. Garrett received word that someone was coming. He advised his men to ready their weapons, that only the men they were seeking would be riding this time of night. Garrett, Chambers, and another man took up a position on the porch of the hospital and hid among some harnesses hanging there.

Horses approached, slow and quiet in the snow. The Kid was in the lead. At one point he decided he wanted a chew of tobacco but had exhausted his supply. He pulled out of the line and rode to the rear of the column to get one from Wilson. Tom Folliard and Tom Pickett were now in the lead. Folliard rode up to the porch as Garrett yelled, "Halt!" and both the sheriff-elect and Chambers fired their weapons. Folliard's horse was spooked by the blasts, reared, spun on its hind feet, and bolted away at a full gallop. Garrett jacked another round into his Winchester and fired at Pickett, who was also galloping away. Chambers fired at the remaining fleeing riders. All escaped save for Folliard.

Nearly everything that has ever been written about this event and related segments of New Mexico history refers to this man as Tom O'Folliard. As a result of an investigation of genealogical and census records, detective Steve Sederwall learned that his real name was Thomas O. Folliard, the name by which he is referred throughout this book.

Prior to the Civil War, Tom Folliard, a resident of Ireland, immigrated to the United States. He met and married Sarah Cook, and two and a half years later had a son, Thomas O. Folliard. Following the Civil War the elder Folliard moved the family to Monclova in the Mexican state of Coahuila. There Tom Senior and Sarah fell victim to smallpox and died. Thomas, a small baby, was taken in by a native family and raised until such time as members of his own family could retrieve him.

John Cook, Sarah's uncle, took young Thomas back to his home in Uvalde, Texas. The Uvalde census for 1870 lists "Thomas Folliard, 9 years old." Others in the household included David and Eliza Jane Cook, the parents of Sarah. David was identified as a farmer and stock raiser. This would make Eliza Jane Cook, the woman who raised him, Tom's grandmother. Eliza Jane's married name was McKinney; she was Kip McKinney's cousin. Kip McKinney and Tom Folliard were related. McKinney went on to become one of Pat Garrett's deputies.

Folliard was raised in Uvalde, Texas. Pat Garrett also lived in Uvalde between 1891 and 1900. Kip McKinney was from Uvalde. During the 1870s, Uvalde had a population of less than one hundred; thus it is well within the realm of reason to speculate that Garrett, McKinney, and Folliard were all acquainted with one another.

Thalis Cook, son of David and Eliza Jane Cook and Folliard's uncle, was in the Texas Rangers. Thalis wrote to Tom telling him that he was going to come to New Mexico and visit. In a letter found in the Robert N. Mullin Collection, Mrs. O. L. Shipman wrote that the Kid intercepted Thalis's letter and sent Tom away. "The Kid met Uncle Thalis and told him he could not have Tom. Realizing the hopelessness of his mission, Thalis returned to Texas."

Had Thalis been able to talk with Tom Folliard and convince him to return to Texas, history might have turned out differently.

Folliard, badly wounded by the bullets from the weapons of Garrett and Chambers, managed to rein up his horse. Slumped over the saddle, he was crying. He called out to Garrett not to shoot, saying, "I'm killed." Posse members pulled Folliard from his saddle, carried him inside the building, and laid him on a blanket. He lived for another forty-five minutes before expiring. Folliard was only twenty-two years old.

During his final moments Folliard was in great pain. Before he died, he spoke to the sheriff, saying, "If you're a friend, you'll kill me."

In his book Garrett acknowledged Folliard's request. Garrett wrote, "If I was a friend of his I would put him out of his misery. . . . I told him I was no friend of men of his kind who sought to murder me because I tried to do my duty, and I did not shoot up my friends as he was shot."

While historians and writers have passed over Garrett's words with no comment, the fact is that his very words draw the immediate attention of the investigator. Garrett was stressing the business of friends a bit too hard, as if he were trying to cover up the fact that he and Folliard had been friends at one time. And why would Folliard use the words "a friend" to Garrett? To the investigator, this represents another tell.

A few seconds before passing, Folliard asked Barney Mason to have Kip McKinney write to his grandmother in Texas and inform her of his death. This request raises questions: Why did Folliard choose McKinney? Was it because they were kin? Was McKinney nearby, riding with the posse? And how would McKinney know where to write to Folliard's grandmother? In these few words spoken by Folliard and Garrett, there is a mystery, one that invites a solution.

Chapter Ten

THE STINKING SPRINGS INCIDENT

The killing of Tom Folliard demonstrated to Billy the Kid and his gang just how much Pat Garrett and his posse were closing in. After fleeing the scene, the outlaws traveled to the Wilcox Ranch, where they hid out. They knew Garrett's pursuit would not lessen.

Billy the Kid, Charlie Bowdre, Dave Rudabaugh, Billy Wilson, and Tom Pickett were not convinced they could trust rancher Wilcox, but they had few options. On the morning of December 21, they sent Manuel Brazel, co-owner of the ranch, into Fort Sumner to check on Garrett's activities and report back to them. On arriving in town, Brazel approached Garrett and informed him that the men he was looking for were at the ranch. Garrett told Brazel to ride back and tell the Kid that he was still at Fort Sumner with only a few men and was afraid to leave. Brazel decided to spend the night and leave for the ranch in the morning.

The next morning, December 22, as Brazel prepared to leave, Garrett told him to remain at the ranch if the Kid was there. If not, he was to return to Fort Sumner and report. Garrett stated that if Brazel did not return, he and the posse would start for the ranch at two a.m. Brazel reported back to Garrett at midnight on December 23. According to Garrett, "There was snow on the ground, it was desperately cold, and Brazel's beard was full of icicles."

Brazel told Garrett that the Kid and his gang ate dinner at the ranch, mounted up, and rode away. Garrett ordered his posse to saddle up, that they were going to the Wilcox Ranch. Brazel rode with them. After determining for certain that the outlaws had not returned to the ranch, Garrett picked up their trail in the snow and followed it. He was convinced that his quarry was headed for Stinking Springs.

Stinking Springs was a seep spring not far from the Yerby Ranch and Taiban Creek. Near the spring was an old and abandoned rock house where Garrett thought the gang would seek shelter from the storm and cold. The house was described by posse member Charlie Siringo as being twenty feet by thirty feet.

At three a.m. Garrett and his posse reined up four hundred yards from the rock house. Leaving their horses in the charge of Juan Roibal, the lawmen slid their rifles from the saddle scabbards and advanced toward the building. Garrett divided his force, with the two halves approaching each side of the house. Three horses were tied outside the building, saddled. The posse knew they were trailing five men, who they assumed were inside, along with the other two horses.

Garrett instructed some of his posse men to slip up to the house and get the drop on the outlaws inside. They refused, so the lawmen waited in the cold for the three and a half hours remaining until daylight. Garrett's plan was simple: "I told the posse that, should the Kid make his appearance, it was my intention to kill him, and the rest would surrender."

Garrett knew that the Kid was wearing a wide-brimmed, light-colored felt hat with an artistically braided band around the crown. Cal Polk, one of the posse men, said, "We put some blankets down on the snow under the bow of the hill and lay down on them. We could raise our heads one foot and see rite [*sic*] in the front door."

Inside the rock house the first to awaken was Charlie Bowdre. He started a small fire, picked up a nosebag, and stepped outside to feed his horse. He was wearing a hat similar to the Kid's. According to posse member Polk, "Pat told him to throw up his hands." Bowdre turned from his horse, "jerked out 2 pistols and fired." He was immediately struck by three bullets: one on the leg and two in the body. Badly wounded, Bowdre turned and stumbled back into the building.

All was quiet for several minutes. Billy Wilson called out to Garrett that Bowdre was "killed and wanted to come out." Garrett responded, explaining that Bowdre needed to come out with his hands up. According to Garrett, the Kid grabbed the mortally wounded Bowdre by the pistol belt and yanked his weapon around in front so he could pull it. Garrett claimed that the Kid told Bowdre: "They have murdered you, Charlie, but you can get revenge. Kill some of the sons-of-bitches before you die." The Kid then shoved the dying man out the door. It remains unclear how Garrett determined that the Kid made such a statement, if he did at all.

Once out the door, Bowdre stumbled toward the posse, his hands in the air, "and strangling with blood." Garrett caught him as he started to fall, the outlaw whispering, "I wish . . . I wish . . . I wish."

Charlie Bowdre died on a blanket moments later. He was thirty-two years old. Like Folliard four days earlier, he was killed by lawmen from ambush.

Garrett now had the rock house surrounded. He tried to talk the Kid and the others into giving up, but the outlaws were having none of it. The posse heard the sound of digging. One of them, Louis Bousman, said, "Billy and his outfit began trying to dig portholes in that rock building. There was only one north window and one west door. Pat said, 'There is no use for us to lay there all day, we better get away before they do get portholes.'"

Late in the afternoon Billy the Kid told Garrett that they would all come out and surrender. Tom Pickett exited the building waving a white cloth in his right hand. He was followed by Billy Wilson and Dave Rudabaugh. The Kid did not come out. The posse waited for several minutes, and then the Kid announced he was coming out.

According to Paco Anaya, "It was already very late when Billy gave up, and as soon as Billy was secure, Pat went into the house to bring what they had there, and found that Billy had piled up all the rifles and pistols, as well as the gun belts, and did his business on them and got them all covered."

Between the time the others surrendered and the Kid came out of the building, Billy had placed all of the weapons, along with gun belts and holsters, in a pile in a corner of the rock house and urinated on them. If Garrett wanted them, then he could clean them.

But there is more to this tactic than meets the eye. With this act, according to Sederwall, the Kid revealed a tell, something else that researchers throughout the years have missed.

On the night Billy the Kid and his gang arrived at the rock house, they pulled the saddlebags from the saddles, pulled their rifles from the scabbards, and left their mounts tied and saddled. At Fort Sumner they had ridden into an ambush. They knew Garrett and his men were in pursuit, and they wanted to be ready to mount up and leave at a moment's notice. The Kid even led his mare inside the rock house.

What the historians recorded over the years was the obvious: Garrett and his posse arrived at the rock house, surrounded it, killed Bowdre, and left the rest of the gang inside with few options. The Kid gave up. But according to Sederwall, what the historians and writers missed was one of the reasons Garrett was chasing the Kid in the first place. Sederwall pointed out that in addition to pursuing the man who was convicted of killing Sheriff Brady and gunning down two of his deputies, Garrett was sent by the United States Secret Service in pursuit of counterfeiters.

If the Kid and his gang were caught with counterfeit money, the US government would have filed federal counterfeiting charges against them. Consider this: Five outlaws in possession of counterfeit bills were surrounded, trapped inside a rock house with no way out other than to surrender. They had a serious problem. They did not want to be caught in possession of the money. They had a fire going and could have burned the money, but if they did so, then they would lose it. They would have wanted to hide it on the chance that they might be able to return later and retrieve it. But where to hide it?

Garrett's posse heard the sounds of digging and concluded that the gang was digging portholes from which they intended firing upon the posse. There are three elements to this observation that reveal how dreadfully wrong it was. First, the house was made of rock; they were not going to be able to dig through rock. Second, since it was clear that the Kid and his gang were going to have to surrender to the posse, it made no sense that they would have gone to the trouble to dig portholes. Third, portholes were never found in the building and are never mentioned again in the historical record. The Kid and his gang were *not* digging portholes—they were digging a hole in the dirt floor of the rock house in which to bury the counterfeit money.

There is even more evidence for this conclusion. Following the Kid's later escape from the law, he encountered John P. Meadows. As recounted in his book *Pat Garrett and Billy the Kid as I Knew Them: Reminiscences of John P. Meadows*, Meadows suggested to the Kid that he leave for Mexico. The Kid told him, "I haven't any money. I have to go back and get a little before I can leave." This is another tell.

Note that the Kid did not say he had to go back and "make" a little money, or "steal" a little money. He said he had to "go back and get a little" money. He was referring to the money he had cached in the rock house.

Consider this: If a hole was dug and the money buried, the fresh-turned earth would have been easy to spot. The tell is, in fact, right there in the stories of Garrett and the posse members. The Kid, or one of his men, dug a hole, the sounds of the excavation loud enough to be heard and leading the posse men to believe the outlaws were digging portholes. When the hole was dug, the Kid placed a Colt .45 revolver with a five-and-a-half-inch barrel into the sack with the money and buried it. His idea, it can be assumed, was that if he managed to escape later, he could return to this location and retrieve both money and weapon.

In order to camouflage the newly excavated hole, Billy the Kid piled atop it all of the gang's rifles and handguns as well as holsters and gun belts. This done, he urinated on the pile. According to Paco Anaya, when Garrett entered the rock house and saw the pile of weapons still rank with fresh urine, he turned to the Kid and said, "What did you do that to the weapons for?" The Kid replied, "That's all they're good for when you can't use them."

In truth, according to investigator Sederwall, the urine-soaked weapons were good for something: They were hiding the hole in which the counterfeit money was buried. Garrett had been tricked.

The Colt .45 revolver that was buried in a corner of the Stinking Springs cabin by Billy the Kid in 1880
STEVE SEDERWALL COLLECTION

There is yet more evidence for this ruse. In 1932, Tom Pickett, one of the Kid's gang who was captured at Stinking Springs, was living in Arizona. By this time he was elderly and living on a small pension he received from serving sixteen months in a Texas Ranger battalion. According to author Phillip J. Rasch, Pickett grew desperately short of money, so "he sent Ed Coles to dig up a lot of money which the Kid's gang had buried under the floor before their surrender at Stinking Springs. Cole found the spot, but the money was all paper and had all rotted away."

It is possible, probable, that the money did not rot away at all. It is more likely that the Kid had returned to the site and retrieved it.

There is more. Five months elapsed from the time the Kid was arrested at Stinking Springs until his return to Fort Sumner. Logic suggests that, following his return, it would have been an ideal time to retrieve the money. Assume for a moment that the Kid made his way back to the rock house and dug up the money and the Colt .45 he had buried there earlier. Having lain in the ground for five months, the handgun more than likely displayed some rust. Since by this time it can be assumed that the Kid was well armed, the rusted revolver lacked importance, so he tossed it back into the hole and shoved dirt back on top of it.

In the summer of 1910, nine-year-old Ralph Camp was digging in a corner of the old rock house. Only a few inches below the surface, he found a rusted, and still loaded, Colt .45.

Chapter Eleven

SENTENCED TO HANG

On April 13, 1881, in the Mesilla, New Mexico, courthouse, Billy the Kid rose and, flanked by his attorneys John D. Bail and Albert Jennings Fountain, faced Judge Warren Bristol to learn his fate. Four days earlier the jury had declared the defendant "guilty of murder in the first degree and do assess his punishment at death." The Kid had been found guilty of killing Sheriff William Brady, though no evidence was ever presented to suggest that this was fact.

The Kid had been tried as "William Bonney, alias William Antrim, alias Kid Antrim, alias, Kid, alias Billy the Kid." Unknown to anyone at the time, neither of these was his real name. Judge Bristol ordered the Kid to be remanded into the custody of the Lincoln County sheriff and for the deputies to transport him back to the town of Lincoln, where, on May 13, 1881, between the hours of ten a.m. and three p.m., the county sheriff was to find a place of his choosing and hang the prisoner by the neck until dead.

In appearance, Billy the Kid did not have the look of a feared and notorious outlaw. A few weeks earlier Texas Ranger J. B. Gillett saw him and described him as an "almost child-like boy." Gillett further stated that the Kid "was far from a bad looking man, looked just like an ordinary cowboy . . . and all most [*sic*] feminine in appearance."

During a stop in Las Vegas, New Mexico, as the Kid was being transported to Mesilla, a reporter for the *Las Vegas Gazette* who saw him wrote: "There was nothing very mannish about him in appearance, for he looked and acted a mere boy . . . looking like a schoolboy, with the traditional silky fuzz on his upper lip, clear blue eyes . . . light hair and complexion."

At twenty years of age, Billy the Kid displayed physical features more commonly used to describe adolescent boys between the ages of ten and fifteen. According to prominent endocrinologist Dr. J. M. Tanner, the developmental stages associated with sexual maturity are not necessarily related to chronological age. The Kid was displaying features associated with Tanner's Sexual Maturity Rating 2. If Billy the Kid at age twenty was displaying SMR2 characteristics, he was, according to Tanner, exhibiting delayed sexual maturity. The Kid's physical appearance as manifested in these descriptions provided by observers will become important later when an investigation of the body of the man Sheriff Pat Garrett shot and killed is conducted.

On April 15, Doña Ana County sheriff James W. Fourtion placed a warrant in the hands of Deputy Robert Olinger. The warrant ordered the deputy to deliver the prisoner, Billy the Kid, to the sheriff of Lincoln County. Olinger was accompanied by several other lawmen. All along the route Olinger, a mean-spirited brute of a man, bullied and threatened the Kid with death. On April 21, Olinger passed the convicted outlaw into the custody of Sheriff Pat Garrett. The Kid was delivered to the Lincoln County Courthouse and placed in the jail located on the second floor. Both the jail and courthouse were housed in the two-story building that was the former Murphy-Dolan Store. The jail had no bars; arrested felons were chained to eyebolts secured in the floor. There were a few other prisoners in the jail that day, and all were guarded by at least three deputies, including Robert Olinger and James Bell.

Lincoln County deputy Robert Olinger
STEVE SEDERWALL COLLECTION

Chapter Twelve

ESCAPE

Billy the Kid's dramatic escape from the Lincoln County Courthouse has been written about hundreds of times in books and articles and offered up in numerous films and features. Almost everyone knows the version of the event as it was originally related by Pat Garrett in the 1882 book *The Authentic Life of Billy the Kid*, which carries his name as the author, a version that has been repeated throughout the decades with little to no variation. An investigation into the reporting of the escape launched by Steve Sederwall revealed elements of this gripping event that had long escaped the notice of earlier researchers and writers.

Consider these truths: (1) Pat Garrett was not present during the Kid's escape; he recreated the event, which took place during his absence, and did so without conducting an appropriate investigation. (2) Almost every writer who has treated this episode has relied on Garrett's version of events. Evidence, however, reveals that Garrett was either mistaken or was deliberately coloring the truth. In either case he was wrong in his assessment of what had occurred, and as a result, all of those who invoked his version over the years were likewise in error.

On being returned to Lincoln, Billy the Kid was taken to the second-floor jail. He was handcuffed, and a set of leg irons was secured around his ankles. The leg irons had been welded closed and were attached to a chain that was bolted to the floor-boards. The guards assigned to him were James Bell and Robert Olinger. Olinger, an overweight forty-year-old hard case from Ohio, had a history of bullying, and stories circulated about him shooting men in the back. The threatening treatment Olinger had accorded the Kid on the trip from Mesilla continued after their arrival in Lincoln.

Originally from Georgia, James W. Bell was a resident of White Oaks, New Mexico, and a former Texas Ranger. On April 4 the Lincoln County Commissioners authorized warrant number 401, which provided Bell the status of special constable and paid him $65.60. Bell's assignment was to guard the Kid until May 13, the date for his hanging. In addition to Billy the Kid, the two guards had charge of five other prisoners, all of whom were involved in an earlier killing in Tularosa. Garrett was not present. The day before the escape, April 27, Garrett rode to Las Tablas, then on to White Oaks for the stated purpose of collecting taxes.

On April 28, Olinger escorted the Tularosa prisoners across the street to the Wortley Hotel for supper. Garrett did not want the Kid unbolted from the floor except to visit the latrine behind the building. Olinger planned to bring a lunch back to the Kid. Until then the outlaw was guarded only by Bell.

According to Garrett, and a version oft repeated, the Kid told Bell he needed to go to the outhouse. Bell unbolted the leg irons from the floor and escorted the prisoner down the only set of stairs connecting the second floor to the first. They went out the west door to the corrals where the outhouse was located, the Kid shuffling along in his irons. The Kid entered the privy while Bell stood guard. When the Kid finished, Bell escorted him back to the courthouse and up the stairs.

According to Pat Garrett:

> *Bell allowed the Kid to get considerably in advance. As the Kid turned on the landing of the stairs, he was hidden from*

> *Bell. He was light and active, and, with a few noiseless bounds, reached the head of the stairs, turned to the right, put his shoulder to the door of the room used as an armory (though locked this door was known to open by a firm push), entered, seized a six-shooter, returned to the head of the stairs just as Bell faced him on the landing of the stair-case, some twelve steps beneath, and fired. Bell turned, ran out into the corral and towards the little gate. He fell dead before reaching it.*

The landing referred to by Garrett was "five or six steps" up from the first floor. During one of the remodeling phases of the courthouse, this landing was later modified such that it was only one step up.

The Kid slipped his handcuffs, stated Garrett, and went to the armory and grabbed Olinger's double-barreled shotgun. Olinger had loaded the gun that morning in the presence of the Kid, placing eighteen buckshot in each barrel. Olinger allegedly told the Kid, "The man that gets one of these loads will feel it." With the shotgun the Kid returned to the guardroom and stationed himself at the east window.

After hearing the shot that killed Bell, Olinger, in the company of Luther M. Clements, ran from the Wortley Hotel, crossed the street, and passed through a front gate. By the time Olinger reached a point between the gate and the courthouse, he was stopped by the sound of the Kid's voice from the second-story window when he allegedly said, "Hello, old boy."

The Kid pulled the trigger on the shotgun, sending the buckshot into Olinger's "right shoulder and breast and side." The deputy fell dead.

According to Pat Garrett, the Kid then ordered Gottfried Gauss (Garrett wrote his name as Geiss), who was employed to work at the building, to saddle a horse in a nearby stable that belonged to Billy Burt, the probate clerk, and bring it to him. While this was being done, the Kid went to the front window, where he had a commanding view of the street, and "filed the shackles from one leg." He exited the building, mounted the horse, and rode out of town toward the west.

While in White Oaks, Garrett received a note from John C. Delaney reporting the escape of the Kid. The sheriff hastened back to Lincoln. On arriving, he found his two dead deputies, who by this time had been placed in a wooden shed behind the courthouse.

Across the decades since 1881, it has been Pat Garrett's description of what took place at the Lincoln County Courthouse during the escape of Billy the Kid that has been hammered into history with little to no challenge. After well over a century of telling and retelling, as well as writing and rewriting about this event, it is Garrett's version, as written by his friend Ashmon Upson, that has prevailed and been regarded as the authoritative one, i.e., the accepted history. Author J. C. Dykes maintained that *The Authentic Life* "has been standard source material for many writers down through the years and one of the books . . . most frequently quoted." Dykes goes on to state, "Yet . . . this book . . . is responsible for the perpetuation of unverified tales" about the life of Billy the Kid. It was the repetition of Garrett's account that predominated, not research, and certainly not investigation. It is the constant repetition, without investigation by so-called historians and writers, that has propelled Garrett's version to the forefront.

Maurice Garland Fulton, one of the first historians to study the Kid's escape and the first to cast some doubt on Garrett's version, presented three theories about what may have taken place. The first theory was based on Walter Noble Burns's book *The Saga of Billy the Kid* (1926), which has the outlaw snatching Bell's pistol while the two are playing a card game called monte.

The second theory is Garrett's. Since Garrett was the sheriff at the time, this has come to be known as the "official" explanation of the escape and the murders of Olinger and Bell.

The third theory originates from Fulton himself. He contended that one of the Kid's friends left a pistol in the outhouse and when the Kid reached the top of the stairs he turned on Bell with the gun; Bell "turned and ran," leaving the Kid no choice but to shoot the fleeing deputy.

In addition to Fulton's theories, there are at least two additional versions of what took place at the courthouse. One is the testimony of William Henry Roberts, aka Billy the Kid, as related in *Billy the Kid: Beyond the Grave* (2005) and *Billy the Kid: The Lost Interviews* (2012). The other is related to the findings of a crime scene investigation conducted by Steve Sederwall.

Why so many theories? The truth is, each of Fulton's theories is little more than conjecture. Walter Noble Burns's book was described as a "set of fantasies" by author Jon Tuska. While somewhat loosely based on history, *The Saga of Billy the Kid* is, in fact, a novel filled with fictional dialogue and events and disguised as a work of history. No enlightened historian takes it seriously.

The description of the Kid's escape that appears in Garrett's book, *The Authentic Life of Billy the Kid*, is fraught with questionable observation and spurious conclusion. This publication was characterized by writer Frederick Nolan as filled with "many inaccuracies, evasions, and even untruths" and a "farrago of nonsense." A thorough and intensive examination of Garrett's life reveals the record of a man known to color the truth, to put it kindly, particularly if it made him appear more important, and more courageous. After all, Garrett was a politician.

Compared to Burns's and Garrett's versions, Garland's theory has greater plausibility but still contains flaws. However, only two people—Billy the Kid and Deputy James Bell—were present at the time. Bell did not live long enough to provide any testimony.

According to William Henry Roberts, aka Billy the Kid, in *Billy the Kid: The Lost Interviews*, he asked Bell to take him to the latrine. When the deputy went to a nearby room to obtain the key to unlock the leg irons, the Kid slipped his right hand from the cuffs. When Bell approached with the key, the Kid swung the loose cuff, striking the deputy in the back of the head several times. When Bell fell to the floor, the Kid grabbed his gun and ordered him to accompany him to the armory. On the way Bell decided to run and headed straight for the stairway. Not wanting Bell to alert Olinger, the Kid shot him as he ran down the steps.

Some Billy the Kid lore has the outlaw firing two shots at Bell. One version has the second round missing the deputy and striking the wall at the first landing. Another version maintains that the bullet that struck Bell passed through his body and struck the wall. To this day, what has been described by many as a bullet hole can still be seen on this wall, evidence, they claim, of the violence. This is yet another Billy the Kid myth, one that has been repeated so often that it, too, has become part of the legend. No matter how hard a legend is defended, however, it does not change the facts, which lead, in turn, to the truth.

There exists no evidence that the Kid fired more than one shot. Gottfried Gauss was quoted as saying, "I heard a shot fired." One shot. Since 1881, when Deputy Bell was killed, the inside stairs down which Bell fled were replaced, the landing changed, and the walls replastered. It is logical to assume that a bullet hole in a wall would have been plastered over.

There also exists a problem with the geography of the setting. Today, the so-called bullet hole appears to be chest high relative to a man the size of Bell standing on the landing. If, however, we consider the location of the landing in 1881—five or six steps up from the first floor—then the bullet, if fired by the Kid, would have struck at a level closer to Bell's ankles, not his chest.

The bullet hole myth is a canard, and one that a number of area residents claimed was perpetrated by Lincoln County War historian Maurice G. Fulton. A long-held and so-called Lincoln secret is that Fulton placed the hole in the wall himself with a hand drill.

Crimes were committed in the Lincoln County Courthouse on April 28, 1881—two murders and a jailbreak. Yet no formal investigation was ever made, not even by the man who had the responsibility to do so—Sheriff Pat Garrett. Some research has been applied to the event, all of it relying heavily on Garrett's version of what happened. Going beyond research and applying modern crime-solving and investigative techniques to this case was long overdue. It was just the thing that captured the interest of Sederwall, who determined that such an investigation was necessary. Some might argue that such a thing cannot be done in the case of an event that occurred over a century earlier. They would be wrong. Virtually every cold case contains new information if new eyes search and a fresh and open mind considers the evidence.

Chapter Thirteen

LINCOLN COUNTY COURTHOUSE CRIME SCENE INVESTIGATION

To many, Sheriff Pat Garrett was and is a hero. Some western history/lawmen enthusiasts continue to hold Garrett up as a daring law enforcement officer and view him as the man who doggedly pursued the outlaw Billy the Kid and reputedly took him down. To this day, members of the Lincoln County Sheriff's Department wear a shoulder patch on their uniform sleeves that bears an image of Garrett.

Insightful and curious people, however, have long been bothered by Garrett's accounts in his book, *The Authentic Life of Billy the Kid*. One account in particular describes the young outlaw's escape from the Lincoln County jail but is fraught with inconsistencies and spurious inclusions. Garrett provided seemingly precise detail of the event, though he was not present. In his story Garrett stated that he elicited information from Gottfried Gauss, a building employee, though Garrett could not even get his name correct. It has been established that Gauss was not an eyewitness to anything that took place inside the courthouse.

Steve Sederwall's cop instinct kicked into gear on studying Garrett's account of the escape, and he determined that a number of the lawman's statements are suspicious and deserve to be addressed.

Garrett stated that the Kid ascended the staircase ahead of Bell

> *with a few noiseless bounds, reached the head of the stairs, turned to the right, put his shoulder to the door of the room used as an armory (though locked, this door was well known to open by a firm push), entered, and seized a six-shooter, returned to the head of the stairs just as Bell faced him on the landing of the stair-case, some twelve steps beneath, and fired.*

First, one has to wonder how Garrett arrived at this scenario since he was miles away in White Oaks at the time. Second, the sheriff would have us believe that the Kid, his ankles linked by leg irons, was capable of making "a few noiseless bounds." Such a notion is absurd. It is well known that Garrett's friend and drinking buddy Ashmon Upson wrote most, if not all, of *The Authentic Life*. Statements such as the one about "noiseless bounds" makes one wonder if Garrett ever actually read the book before it was published. No competent lawman would ever allow such a thing to appear in print.

Garrett's comment about the armory door being "known to open by a firm push" reveals a lot. Garrett had the most desperate outlaw in the American West in his custody, along with some other prisoners, on the second floor of the courthouse with an armory door "known to open by a firm push." If Garrett, the chief law enforcement officer in charge of a noted criminal, was telling the truth, he left loaded guns in an armory knowing the door was easily opened. For a seasoned lawman such a thing is incomprehensible.

Garrett was not finished. He attempted to remove any responsibility from himself by stating, "Yet, in self-defense, and hazarding the charge of shirking responsibility and laying it upon dead men's shoulders, I must say that my instructions to caution and the routine of duty were not heeded and followed." Garrett takes no responsibility for the killings and the escape. Instead, he lays the blame "upon dead men's shoulders."

Garrett's description of the escape was the one oft quoted and referred to by subsequent writers and historians, but the truth is, an investigation of the escape and killing of the two deputies was never made at the time, a serious breach of process and protocol by the county sheriff. Sederwall saw an opportunity to remedy the situation nearly one and a quarter centuries later, on August 4, 2004. On the afternoon of that day, Sederwall, accompanied by a contingent of New Mexico lawmen, along with forensic specialist Dr. Henry Lee of Connecticut, met in front of the Lincoln County Courthouse. Lee was one of the foremost forensic scientists in the country at the time and had his own television show.

Sederwall determined that it was necessary to examine the stairs and the landing where Billy the Kid shot Deputy James Bell. There was a possibility that traces of Bell's blood might still be found.

Dr. Henry Lee and investigator Steve Sederwall
STEVE SEDERWALL COLLECTION

Under the stairwell and the second-floor landing, brown stains from years of mopping were found. Mop water had seeped through cracks and stained the underside of the wooden boards. Sederwall later determined that the staircase had been replaced and was not the same one that the Kid and Bell traveled up and down in 1881. The investigators moved to the top of the stairs and the landing. After the release of the movie *Young Guns II*, tourists flocked to Lincoln. The increased traffic on the second floor of the courthouse, a New Mexico State Monument, prompted state officials to put down plywood walkways to protect the old wooden floorboards.

By the time Sederwall and his team reached the second floor, the plywood had been removed, exposing the original floorboards. The Kid, Bell, Olinger, and Garrett had walked on these same boards. After an initial examination Dr. Lee determined that some of the floorboards were newer than others and the landing consisted of wood planks of different ages.

Dr. Lee explained that he would be performing "presumptive blood tests" and prepared a Q-tip. o-Tolidine, a chemical test reagent for blood, would be employed. Lee worked slowly, meticulously, and deliberately, swabbing the cracks between the boards and under the edge of the second-floor landing. After each swab he carefully placed a drop of a chemical on the head of the Q-tip, turning it blue. "Positive for blood," he said. The tests showed positive reactions for blood in several areas on the landing. The underside of the landing was also tested, and locations of blood residue were logged and mapped.

Dr. Lee's conclusion was that "chemical tests for the presence of blood were positive with some of [the floorboard] stains."

A thorough examination of Lincoln County Courthouse records by Sederwall revealed only one instance where blood was shed in the building, and that occurred during the escape of Billy the Kid and the shooting of Deputy James Bell. Dr. Lee had found evidence of Bell's blood on the second-floor landing, a significant amount of it. The evidence indicated that Bell bled heavily at this location. With this information in hand, it was time for another look at Pat Garrett's interpretation of what happened in the courthouse.

Garrett wrote that the Kid retrieved a handgun and faced Bell, who was "on the [first-floor] landing of the stair-case, some twelve steps beneath." Garrett, having no idea what happened, merely concocted this scenario. How could he have known what step or steps Bell was standing on? When Garrett returned to Lincoln from White Oaks and looked over the crime scene, assuming he did, he could not possibly have missed the blood on the boards of the second-floor landing. The blood was obvious, and there was a lot of it. How do we know? Regard the following.

Gottfried Gauss, a fifty-eight-year-old German immigrant and former priest, was outside the courthouse when Billy the Kid shot Bell. Gauss was quoted in the *White Oaks Leader* on January 15, 1890, as stating, "That memorable day I came out of my room, whence I had gone to light my pipe, and was crossing the yard behind the courthouse, when I heard a shot fired, a tussle upstairs in the courthouse, somebody hurrying down stairs, and deputy-sheriff Bell emerging from the door running toward me." Gauss's recollections placed Bell "upstairs," or on the second-floor landing, and "hurrying downstairs."

Sederwall subsequently learned that Sophie Poe, wife of Lincoln County sheriff John Poe, who was elected in 1882, provided some pertinent information on where Bell may have been standing when he was shot. John Poe took office in January 1883, and in June of that year, he and wife Sophie took up residence in one of the empty rooms of the courthouse. Mrs. Poe wrote in her book, *Buckboard Days*, that there was "one feature of the new home which I did not enjoy." She was referring to the bloodstains she encountered on the staircase and the second-floor landing, stains that were "a grim reminder of the day two years before, when Billy the Kid had shot and killed his guard, James W. Bell."

She noted that the bloodstains indicated that Bell "had fallen to the bottom of the stairs." Fallen from where? Clearly, Bell fell, or stumbled, and bled from the top of the stairs down to the first-floor landing. How is it that Sophie Poe could see then what Garrett could not see two years and two months earlier when the blood was relatively fresh? Garrett claimed that Bell never reached the top of the stairs. Both stories cannot be true.

Gauss had no reason to lie, to fabricate what he heard. Sophie Poe likewise had no reason to lie. Both of their accounts contradict that of Sheriff Pat Garrett. Was Garrett so dense that he could not interpret the crime scene accurately? Was it possible Garrett did not see the bloodstains on the second-floor landing? The answer to both of these questions is a resounding NO. Garrett was either lying or grossly incompetent. As a seasoned law enforcement officer, Garrett had experience, was known to be wily, and should have possessed sufficient investigative skills; thus, incompetence should be ruled out. If Garrett was lying about what took place, the question of "why" must be asked. Garrett would have no reason to concoct a story regarding the escape unless he was attempting to cover up his gross inefficiency or he was culpable in some manner.

When seeking the truth of what happened at the Lincoln County Courthouse, investigator Sederwall determined that it was necessary to set the filter of myth aside and deal with the principals as real men, reacting and responding to the situation as real men would do. When a focus is applied to the evidence and not the myth, it becomes clear that Pat Garrett's version of what occurred must be wrong.

Garrett's statement that the Kid "slipped his handcuffs over his hands" needs to be examined. The first question to be asked is: How would Garrett know? Part of the Billy the Kid myth is that because he had small hands and comparatively large wrists, he was equipped to shed cuffs. This myth, however, is likely based on Garrett's interpretation, for prior to the release of *The Authentic Life* there had never been a reference to the Kid performing this trick.

Such a thing was possible, particularly if the cuffs used in 1881 were not fastened tightly. Nearly every policeman who has handled a cuffed prisoner understands how the Kid's cuffs came off. When the Kid asked Bell to escort him to the outhouse, this was similar to requests made by thousands of cuffed prisoners. The Kid's hands were cuffed in front, not behind. With a prisoner's hands are cuffed behind, the arms can become numb and it is impossible to eat. Further, we know that the Kid and Bell had been playing cards or checkers.

If the scenario that has Bell taking the Kid downstairs and outside to the privy is true, they would have paused at the outhouse door. Bell pulled the handcuff key from his pocket, removed the Kid's right cuff, and, if typical lawman protocol was followed, fastened it on his left wrist next to the other cuff. If a prisoner is cuffed with his hands behind his back, he is unable to unbutton his pants. If cuffed in front, he is unable to clean himself properly. The removal of one cuff was partially substantiated by a line in the April 30, 1881, edition of the *Santa Fe New Mexican*: "[Billy the Kid] had shackles on his ankles, and a pair of handcuffs locked on one wrist, leaving one free."

Inside the outhouse, according to one version of events, the Kid found a handgun placed there by a friend and conspirator. When finished with his privy business, he would have placed the weapon in the waistband of his pants and pulled his shirt over the revolver.

Normally a lawman would have recuffed the prisoner when the outhouse duties were finished. If the outhouse scenario was true, then Bell made a mistake in not doing so. Bell, however, was aware that the Kid's ankles were shackled with leg irons and a short chain and that he could not run. After leaving the outhouse, it can be assumed that the Kid proceeded toward the courthouse and Bell simply decided to recuff him when the two returned to the second floor.

A question that begs to be asked is: Why did the Kid not shoot Bell on stepping out of the outhouse? One answer is that Bell and the Kid, while not good friends, were at least friendly to one another. In contrast with Olinger, who tormented, intimidated, and threatened the Kid, Bell treated the Kid well. Additional insight was provided by John P. Meadows on February 26, 1931, during a talk he gave in Roswell. Meadows stated, "What the Kid wanted to do was to make both Bell and Olinger prisoners."

Meadows's comment was substantiated in part by another offered by Maurice G. Fulton: "The Kid and Bell had been on friendly terms and only as a last resort, in self-protection, would the Kid have shot him."

Another question that needed to be addressed was: How did the killing of James Bell occur? According to Sederwall, to answer this, it would be necessary to disregard the myth and turn to the physical evidence and witness testimony. There are two possible scenarios.

Scenario #1 was arrived at as a result of an analysis engineered by Sederwall. It has Billy the Kid climbing the stairs to the second floor of the courthouse with Bell just behind him. As the Kid reached the top of the stairs, with his back toward Bell, he pulled the revolver found in the outhouse from his waistband. Bell was surprised and confused as he tried to process this information. Bell's neuromuscular responses kicked in.

Law enforcement officers are trained in and are well aware of these kinds of situations. David A. Brewer, Homeland Security and senior law enforcement specialist for the Federal Law Enforcement Training Center in Artesia, New Mexico, explained what happened next.

According to Brewer, Bell, climbing the stairs just behind the Kid, "grabbed for the weapon, an action in response to the tunnel vision brought on by the sudden threat of a weapon in his face." In order to grab the weapon, Bell had to lunge forward. The Kid, startled by Bell's action, responded by stepping backward. Because of the leg irons, the Kid stumbled, the finger pressure on the handgun's trigger increased, and the weapon was discharged.

Brewer explains:

> *Most handguns of the period 1881 were single action revolvers. . . . If the weapon were in single-action mode (hammer back) when Deputy Bell grabbed for the weapon, the reflex action would have caused the weapon to discharge (sudden fright response). If there were a struggle over the weapon, a similar result would have occurred (push-pull effect), the weapon would have discharged.*

When Bell leaned forward to grab the weapon, his arm was extended and angled up toward the Kid. Garrett wrote that "Bell was hit under the right arm, the ball passing through the body and coming out under the left arm."

The historical record shows that Bell had large gashes on his head as though he had been beaten. It is possible that when Bell grabbed the Kid's weapon and the two fell to the floor, the Kid may have tried to get the deputy to turn loose by beating him across the head with the cuffs still attached to his left wrist.

Bell was bleeding from his head wounds, and a second or two later was losing blood from a bullet wound in his torso. The blood was pumping out of him and onto the wooden floor, where it was clearly noticed by Sophie Poe twenty-six months later and found again by crime scene investigators in 2004.

Sederwall's crime scene investigation, facilitated by Dr. Henry Lee, revealed that Bell lost a great deal of blood. As a result, Bell grew weak and blackness seeped into his consciousness. His grip on the handgun loosened, and he rose, turned, and stumbled down the stairs, only to die a few moments later. Gauss reported the sounds of a struggle, a gunshot, and Bell staggering down the stairs.

Scenario #2 was provided by William Henry Roberts, aka Billy the Kid. During a 1949 interview Roberts related his version of what happened:

> *I asked Bell to unlock the chain and take me to the latrine. . . . At first he said no, said he didn't know if he should while Bob [Olinger] was across the street. . . . After a little while he went into that room and got the key to unlock his chain.*
>
> *At this moment I slipped my right hand from the cuffs and waited, holding them in my left. Bell came out of the office. . . . and when he came over to me I swung my handcuffs and hit him hard in the back of the head a couple of times. [He] tumbled over on the floor and I grabbed his gun and the key.*
>
> *I told him I would not hurt him if he would do as I said. I told him to . . . unlock the armory so I can get some guns and ammunition and I wanted to lock him in there until I could escape. . . . [He] walked through the office [and when] he stepped into the hall he ran for the stairway. . . . I jumped and skid across the floor. . . Bell was running down the steps . . . I had to shoot him before he . . . warned Olinger. . . . I pulled the trigger too quickly, and the bullet struck the wall on that side. It must have ricocheted and struck him under the arms, coming out on the other side.*

Like the first scenario, Roberts's version is plausible. It is well known that head wounds bleed heavily. At the moment Bell reached the landing at the top of the stairs, it is possible that he paused a moment in order to determine the location of the Kid. During this pause copious amounts of blood could have fallen from his head wounds onto the floor, the remnants of which were found by Sederwall and his investigative team a century and a quarter later.

Billy the Kid, in a desperate effort to survive, killed two more men, setting the stage for additional pursuit and confrontation with the law.

Chapter Fourteen

AN ESCAPE PLOT

As investigator Steve Sederwall applied his energies and expertise to the Lincoln County Courthouse crime scene, additional aspects of Billy the Kid's escape surfaced as a result of his analysis of witness testimony as well as additional writings and observations. Already sensitized to Garrett's perfidy, Sederwall examined much of the material with an eye toward encountering further evidence that Garrett had lied, and the possibility that he may have been more involved in the Kid's escape than we have been led to believe.

As mentioned in the previous chapter, Gottfried Gauss was what detectives call an "earwitness" to the escape and shooting of the two deputies, as opposed to an "eyewitness." In his book Garrett accepted Gauss as a witness and wrote, "We have . . . the sparse information elicited from Mr. Geiss [*sic*] . . . to determine the facts in regard to events immediately following Olinger's departure." In spite of this, Garrett related a different story than the one this witness offers.

Though Garrett stated that he had earwitness testimony from Gauss, he did not bother to utilize any of it. Garrett discounted the only witness who told him there was a "tussle upstairs" and then, for reasons known only to him, placed Bell twelve steps down from the second-floor landing.

Garrett claimed that only "one other shot was heard before Olinger appeared on the scene, but it is believed to have been an accidental one by the Kid while prospecting with the arms." Garrett loses credibility with almost every sentence he writes. Was he claiming, then, that the Kid accidentally shot Bell "while prospecting with the arms"? Did Garrett believe readers were going to be convinced that while the Kid was "prospecting with the arms" Bell was simply standing around on the stairs waiting for something to happen? Did he think for one moment that anyone would fall for his explanation that the Kid accidentally fired a round that managed somehow to kill Bell? And when did the Kid have time to go into the armory to prospect with the arms? This entire sequence by Garrett is complete fantasy.

In spite of the testimony provided by Gauss, Garrett concocted his own version of the escape and shootings. Furthermore, he ignored the trail of Bell's blood, evidence that was apparent even two years and two months later. Over the decades researchers and writers have passed over these inconsistencies, but these same contradictions and irregularities are what tempt the conscientious investigator to peel back the layers and try to determine what actually happened. Investigators are suspicious of coincidence, and the sequence of events as described by Garrett is full of coincidence.

Was it a coincidence that Garrett chose to be away from Lincoln on the day of the escape? Was it a coincidence that Gauss, who was working in the garden for most of the day, chose to pause and light his pipe just as Olinger took the five prisoners from the courthouse to the Wortley Hotel? Was it a coincidence that the Kid chose that time to ask Bell to take him to the outhouse? Sederwall's cop instincts suggested to him that there were too many coincidences, and his law enforcement experience alerted him to the notion that the sheer quantity of them was suggestive of a plot.

Mrs. Lesnett of Carrizozo, New Mexico, knew Billy the Kid because he had been a guest in her home. During an interview in 1937, Lesnett stated that she saw the Kid again as a "prisoner guarded by Bell and Olinger. Olinger, knowing that I liked the Kid, gleefully invited me to the hanging. I turned my head and blinked fast to keep back the tears. Suddenly the Kid turned to me and said, 'Mrs. Lesnett, they can't hang me if I'm not there, can they?'"

Two days later the Kid escaped. The above is suggestive of the notion that the Kid may have been aware of a plan to facilitate his escape.

Garrett's trip to White Oaks is suspicious. He wrote that he went to collect taxes, a task for which the sheriff's office was responsible. One has to wonder why he selected that particular time to be away, and why he decided it was necessary for him to undertake this task rather than send a deputy. Remember, Garrett had just captured the most notorious outlaw in the American Southwest, a charismatic youth who had been generating a great deal of newspaper coverage around the state, as well as the American West. Garrett was a political animal—he thrived on newspaper coverage and any other attention he could get. He was the chief law enforcement officer in the county. He could remain in Lincoln and bask in the light of his accomplishment and entertain the press explaining how he captured Billy the Kid. Instead, he left town on a mundane errand. To an investigator, this has the earmarks of creating an alibi. Did Garrett, like Gauss, know about an escape plot? And, more importantly, was he part of it? And if so, why? If such a plan had indeed involved Garrett, then the subsequent implication is that he had set up his own deputies to be murdered.

Garrett wrote that while at White Oaks, he received a letter from John C. Delaney, Esq., of Fort Stanton, merely stating the fact of the Kid's escape and the killing of the guards. Note that Garrett used the word "killing" instead of "murdering." According to Sederwall, this choice of words reveals less of an emotional impact on the learning of this deadly act.

Other statements by Garrett also invite suspicion. To the investigator, he is telling more than he intends. When relating the story of the escape, Garrett said, "We have the Kid's tale." Later he employed the term "the Kid's admissions." When would Garrett have heard the Kid's tale and/or the Kid's admissions? When the sheriff left for White Oaks on April 27, it was the last time he saw the Kid until his claim that he shot him in Fort Sumner almost three months later.

At one point in *The Authentic Life*, Garrett stated, "The Kid afterwards told Peter Maxwell that Bell shot at him twice and just missed him." Why would the Kid say such a thing if it did not happen? By this time Garrett's word has become so untrustworthy that it is difficult to believe anything he says. He is clearly fabricating.

Garrett got caught in other lies related to the Kid's escape. He wrote that, after killing Olinger and Bell, the Kid "ordered the old man [Gauss] to go and saddle a horse that was in the stable, the property of Billy Burt, deputy clerk of probate." Garrett stated that the Kid mounted and "the horse broke loose and ran toward the Rio Bonito." The Kid then sent Andrew Nimley, one of the other five prisoners, to retrieve the horse. This done, the Kid remounted and, according to Garrett, said, "Tell Billy Burt I will send his horse back to him." The Kid then rode away, "the shackles still hanging to one leg."

To the trained investigator, states Sederwall, this has the sound of leading away from the truth. Often when someone is lying they tend to make a bigger deal than necessary out of what they want you to believe. Garrett focused on and made a significant issue out of the horse he claimed the Kid rode during his escape. In Garrett's telling, he entered into a somewhat long and detailed story instead of simply stating that the Kid stole a horse and rode away. He told us who owned the horse, even providing the Kid some dialogue relative to the owner. Throughout history this version of the Kid's escape has him riding away on Billy Burt's horse. The source of this information is Pat Garrett, but once again Garrett was lying.

Gorgonio Wilson was an eyewitness to the killings of Bell and Olinger and the Kid's escape. During an interview published in the August 7, 1955, *El Paso Times*, Wilson, who was eighty-nine years old at the time, stated, "When Billy [the Kid] saw me looking he yelled out of the window of the jail for me to run and tell Goss [*sic*] . . . to go and saddle up Pat Garrett's horse and bring him quick."

Pat Garrett's horse? The sheriff's horse was named Black Mart. Robert L. Corn, in a 1938 interview, is quoted as saying, "The splendid horse named Black Mart . . . was one he sold to Pat Garrett and was used by Billy the Kid when he shot Olinger and made his escape in Lincoln."

Robert Corn's sister, May Corn Marley, stated, "[My father] raised the horse that Billy the Kid made his escape on. . . . Pat Garrett bought him from my father [Martin V. Corn] and named him Black Mart after my father."

After fleeing the town of Lincoln, the Kid rode Black Mart straight to the home of Jesus Padilla, where he met his friend Yginio Salazar. In 1977, Margarita Salazar, Yginio's daughter, was interviewed by her son Joe Salazar and Colleen Garrett for the Lincoln County Historical Society. Margarita Salazar stated, "[Billy the Kid] went on Pat Garrett's horse. The shackles [on his legs] scared the first horse [Gauss] brought and it threw Billy. [Gauss] brought the wrong horse. [Billy] said, 'Bring me Pat Garrett's horse.'"

When Yginio first saw Billy the Kid after the escape, the outlaw, according to Margarita, said, "I've got Pat Garrett's horse and I [want to] send him back." Margarita said her father told her that "Billy wrote a note and put it on Pat's horse. It said, 'Well, Pat, I'm glad that you have your horse back. Your horse is going back where you are at. Thank you for your horse but let me tell you don't forget to keep your promise true. . . . Chase me, too, but you know what you make your promise to.'" Margarita also implied that Yginio was part of the escape plot.

The mention of a promise Garrett made to Billy the Kid is intriguing. What sort of promise could Garrett have made? Was it related to an escape plot? This is yet another mystery that begs attention.

Gottfried Gauss's role and statements are also worthy of examination. Historian and writer Eve Ball, in her book *Ma'am Jones of the Pecos*, stated that "Jim Jones went to Lincoln [to visit Billy the Kid]. The guards would not permit him to see the prisoner, but through his friends he got word to . . . Gauss that he was there to help with Billy's escape. Gauss replied that Billy had plans and that Jim was not to spoil them. He was just to wait."

Based on Ball's statement, Jones knew there was an escape plan in the works and he wanted to be involved, but Gauss cautioned him away. It should be pointed out here that the Kid and Gauss were well acquainted with each other, perhaps even friends; both had worked for John Tunstall at the same time on the Rio Feliz ranch. Furthermore, Gauss had nothing but enmity for Garrett, Murphy, Dolan, and the rest of the Lincoln power structure. His statements relative to such have been documented.

Ball implied that Gauss was in on the plot. Gauss knew when Olinger took the prisoners across the street. He knew when the Kid went into the outhouse and presumably knew he would locate a handgun there. Gauss's comments, added to Ball's statement, indicated a suspicious consistency. At the time, Gauss and Sam Wortley were working in the garden behind the courthouse. On seeing Olinger cross the street with the prisoners, Gauss dropped his hoe and went into his house, as he stated, to light his pipe. His house was located just behind the courthouse. To the trained investigator, this suggests that Gauss realized the escape plot was unfolding and he did not want to be in the middle of it in case there was gunfire. Wortley, who was also likely part of the plot, laid down his hoe and walked away. From his window Gauss then saw Bell take the Kid to the outhouse. If he were in his house lighting his pipe, the only way he would know this would be if he were looking out the window.

Writer Frederick Nolan, a staunch supporter of the myth, even concedes that "it is not at all outside the bounds of possibility that [Gauss] was aware that someone had furnished the Kid with the gun that Billy used to kill Bell."

To investigator Sederwall, there are too many coincidences, too many lies. The evidence suggests there was a plot afoot. The evidence further reveals that little to none of the information provided by Pat Garrett was close to the truth. Could Garrett have been part of the plot? It is clear that Garrett was trying to accomplish two things: (1) Garrett developed for the Kid an image of a ruthless, dangerous outlaw, one who would stop at nothing in order to survive. In this manner he built the Kid up as a most dramatic and threatening opponent, thus making himself, Garrett, look heroic by contrast. (2) Garrett knew he made a huge blunder in leaving Lincoln before the escape, and he attempted to remove responsibility from himself by putting forth nothing but lies in order to cover up his own incompetence, even blaming his own deputies, Bell and Olinger, for mishandling the prisoner.

To what degree, if any, could Pat Garrett have been involved in this plot? His strange reactions to the killing of his deputies invites suspicion. Even though Garrett arrived at the crime scene a day late, any competent lawman would have sealed off the town and questioned anyone and everyone to try to get information. Instead, Garrett remained rather passive about the entire affair. The sheriff completely ignored the blood on the landing and the stairs. Then he lied about the entire scenario leading up to the shooting of Deputy Bell.

Garrett also lied about events related to the escape. Four witnesses stated that they saw Billy the Kid ride out of Lincoln on Garrett's horse, Black Mart, yet Garrett went into unnecessary (and fabricated) detail about how the Kid took the probate clerk's horse. Garrett, by the way, was the only person who advanced the notion that the escape was made on a horse other than his own, yet Garrett's version of the event is the one most referred to by historians and writers. Could it be that this was an attempt by Garrett to throw suspicion off of him and blame others? Given that Garrett had his sights set on higher political office, he could not afford to have citizens consider the notion that he lacked competence.

Forget the myth. The evidence clearly shows that Garrett lied. The evidence also is highly suggestive of a possible role of the sheriff in the escape plot, but to what degree and for what reason remains unclear.

Chapter Fifteen

A LIAR AND A THIEF

The mythology related to Sheriff Pat Garrett portrays him as a stalwart lawman, fighting for law and order, and ultimately ridding the country of one of its most violent and dangerous outlaws. The truth about Pat Garrett is far different. The evidence, without doubt, reveals Garrett to be a liar. He lied about the escape of Billy the Kid from the Lincoln County Courthouse, and in-depth research of the rest of his life reveals him as not only a liar, and possibly a pathological one, but also a deadbeat, a debtor, a drunk, an adulterer, and a con man. As it turns out, according to Steve Sederwall, Garrett was also a thief.

After Billy the Kid escaped from Lincoln on Garrett's horse, the bodies of deputies James Bell and Robert Olinger were carried from where they lay to "a room in the corral of the courthouse." The following day, April 29, an inquest was held and a coroner's jury report made. On May 6, Judge James A. Tomlinson appointed Pat Garrett as the administrator of the estate of Robert Olinger. On May 22, Garrett submitted a signed report to the court on an inventory of the property of his late deputy:

One wallet, papers no value

One shotgun Whitney paten (903) broken no value

One watch, Elgin (979197) value one dollar

One set of clothes no value

On April 21, 1883, nearly two years after Olinger was murdered, Garrett filed the probate papers in Lincoln County to adjudicate the estate of his late deputy. The report stated:

In the matter of the estate of Robert Olinger Deceased

I Pat Garrett Administrator of said estate of Robert Olinger dead do hereby certify that after using due diligence that all the property belonging to said estate that I have been able to find is an account allowed by the county commissioners for work done by said Robert Olinger dead to the amt. of Fifty Dollars ($50.00) in the Lincoln County scrip. Against said estate I hereby present an account for Eighty-Four Dollars ($84.00) for money loaned to said Robert Olinger dead & as there is nothing in remaining belonging to said estate so far as I have been able to ascertain. Therefore I ask for a final settlement of said estate and to be discharged by the Honorable court of any further responsibility therein.

No paperwork substantiating the loan made to Olinger was submitted to the court, only Garrett's word.

Referring to the earlier property inventory, there was no mention by Garrett of any handguns. A short time before his death, Olinger escorted five prisoners to the Wortley Hotel for supper. Before departing the courthouse, he left the shotgun leaning against Garrett's desk. (Some writers have stated that Olinger replaced the weapon in the armory.)

It is not possible that a lawman, either today or in 1881, would escort five prisoners, each arrested in connection with a murder, unarmed. Such a thing is beyond belief or comprehension. Further, it must be pointed out that when Olinger heard the shot fired by the Kid in the courthouse he left the hotel and raced across the street to investigate. Would a lawman intent on an immediate response and investigation of a shooting have hurried to the scene unarmed? Not likely. It is impossible to believe that a deputy, particularly one who was on duty, went unarmed.

Texas Ranger J. B. Gillette encountered the Kid and his guards in a wagon in the spring of 1881. He stated, "On the rear seat sat two guards, one was Bob Olinger. . . . Each of these guards wore a brace of pistols and carried in their hands double barreled shotguns." Olinger was carrying the Whitney, the one later used on him by the Kid. A "brace" of pistols is a pair. Olinger carried two handguns. In her book about Billy the Kid, Bell Hudson said, "Big Bob died with his two .45s in his hands, his beloved shotgun across his body." (Following the shooting of Olinger, the Kid was alleged to have broken the weapon over the windowsill and tossed it down onto the body.)

In spite of the obvious, Garrett never mentioned even one handgun, much less two. No one has ever asked the question: What happened to Olinger's revolvers? Did someone take them? Was it Pat Garrett?

Even more compelling information was learned regarding Olinger's shotgun. Today, this weapon is in the possession of James Earle of College Station, Texas. Earle has provided letters of provenance related to this weapon. One letter was from Hiram Dow of Roswell, an attorney, written to John Boylan, curator of the Old Lincoln Memorial in Lincoln, New Mexico. Dated July 25, 1963, it stated that Dow was the curator of the late J. Smith Lea, who passed away August 25, 1933. Lea owned two "Billy the Kid" guns, one of which was "a Whitleyville ten gauge shotgun serial number 903." This was the same shotgun Garrett listed as being broken and having no value. How did it wind up in the possession of Lea?

In the second paragraph of Dow's letter was the explanation: "In 1884, Pat Garrett gave Mr. J. S. Lea the [shotgun] mentioned above, to deliver to Joseph C. Lea in Roswell. Mr. Garrett gave the [gun] to Joseph Lea out of gratitude for some favors Mr. Lea had granted Mr. Garrett."

Administering an estate, as did Garrett, is a legal matter. In this case he swore to the court in an affidavit. He swore that Olinger's shotgun had "no value." Yet Garrett presented the weapon to Lea "out of gratitude for some favors." Did Garrett pay off a debt? If so, then by extension the shotgun had value. Some would argue that Garrett merely gave Lea a gift of the shotgun for some favors. Why, then, would anyone present the gift of a broken shotgun? And why did Garrett maintain possession of the damaged weapon for three years when, as he claimed, it had no value? The corollary to this argument is that the shotgun had no actual value but did have historical value. That is a key word—value. Garrett, in his affidavit to the probate court, said the weapon had no value. Garrett lied.

Furthermore, Garrett apparently kept the weapon long enough to give it away. Why did he not give it to Olinger's next of kin? Immediate and available next of kin happened to be his brother, Wallace Olinger. This would have been the normal, traditional, and ethical manner of doing things. Instead, Garrett kept the shotgun and then gave it to someone who was not a member of the Olinger family "out of gratitude for some favors." If this matter had been taken to court, Garrett would have been charged with theft.

There is more. Apparently Olinger's shotgun was not the only thing stolen by Garrett. Garrett mentions in the probate statement Olinger's "one set of clothes no value." This strikes the investigative eye as somewhat meticulous, to mention the dead man's clothes that had been riddled with buckshot. Yet there is no mention of Olinger's handguns, his horse, his saddle, hat, boots, nothing. Garrett would have us believe Olinger owned virtually nothing—no money, no tobacco, no bedroll, no belongings at all. The historical record tells us otherwise.

A bit of sleuthing by Sederwall revealed that Olinger did have other possessions. In her book *My Girlhood among the Outlaws*, Lily Casey Klasner wrote that after Olinger's death she "was given his six-shooter, field glasses, and gauntlets." Garrett listed none of these. As administrator of Olinger's estate, it was his responsibility and legal duty to take charge of the dead man's property, to make an accurate accounting to be reported to the court. He swore to the court that Olinger's affairs were handled in a legal and ethical manner. Following this, it became the court's responsibility to disburse the items as listed. The evidence showed that either someone stole Olinger's property and Garrett ignored it or Garrett himself took it. The fact that Garrett was in possession of Olinger's shotgun before giving it away suggests the latter.

It has been proven time and again that Pat Garrett, the chief law enforcement officer in Lincoln County, was a liar. The prevailing evidence provides reason to believe he was also a thief.

Chapter Sixteen

Reluctant Pursuit

By early July 1881, Billy the Kid, having escaped from the Lincoln County jail after killing his two guards, was still at large. Anyone who read a newspaper, however, knew where the outlaw was. The May 12 edition of the *Las Vegas Gazette* reported that "William Bonney, alias Kid, has been seen near Fort Sumner, riding a horse stolen from Bell's ranch." Investigators would call this a clue.

In *The Authentic Life*, Garrett stated that he "stayed home, most of the time, and busied myself about the ranch." What kind of lawman is this? Any law enforcement official with the authority and power Garrett had would have had search parties combing the region looking for the escaped outlaw, a man sentenced to be hanged for murder and one who recently shot down and killed two lawmen. With deputies Bell and Olinger barely cold in the ground and their killer still loose in the neighborhood, the chief law enforcement officer of the county elected, by his own admission, to stay home. Lincoln County citizens watched as Garrett did nothing, and before long they began to question his actions.

Garrett attempted to justify his lack of pursuit. He wrote, "During the weeks following the Kid's escape, I was censured by some for my seeming unconcern and inactivity in the matter of his re-arrest. I was egotistical enough to think I knew my business best, and preferred to accomplish the duty, if possible at all, in my own way. I was constantly, but quietly, at work, seeking sure information and maturing my plans of action."

Seeking "sure information" apparently didn't extend to reading the newspaper or listening to area gossip relating to the fact that the Kid was hanging out in Fort Sumner eighty straight-line miles away to the northeast. In fact, Garrett waited *seventy-seven days* before he made a move to go after the Kid.

Why would Garrett wait so long? To any law enforcement professional, maintains Steve Sederwall, such a delay is unheard of. Could it have been that Garrett was afraid of Billy the Kid? Was he afraid that he might be gunned down like Bell and Olinger had been? The evidence would suggest it was so. Or was Garrett's reluctance to become involved in the pursuit of the outlaw related to the possibility that it could have been that he was part of the escape plot?

The long-awaited manhunt for the Kid has been reconstructed on the basis of accounts provided by Garrett and his deputy John W. Poe. A second deputy, Thomas "Kip" McKinney, remained silent on the pursuit.

In early July 1881, Garrett claimed that he learned about the Kid's presence when he received a reply to a letter he sent to Manuel Brazel of Fort Sumner. Brazel wrote that he had not seen the Kid "but from many indications believed he was still in the country." Author Maurice G. Fulton, however, wrote, "It was Frank Stewart and John W. Poe, detectives for the Panhandle Cattlemen's Association, who accomplished the suppression of the Kid. Garrett seems to have lost his zeal altogether after the Kid's jail break in April, 1881."

Poe's account contradicted Garrett's and agreed with Fulton's assessment. Poe wrote that in early July he encountered a man from Texas who provided him information on the whereabouts of Billy the Kid. The informant said, "The Kid was yet in the country, making his headquarters at Fort Sumner, about a hundred miles distant from White Oaks." When Poe presented this information to Garrett, "the sheriff was much more skeptical as to the truth of the story." It seemed as though everyone in the county knew where the Kid was hiding out, yet Garrett remained reluctant to enter into pursuit, or even to examine the information. It was only after Poe's continuous encouragement that Garrett agreed to take up the chase.

One reason the Kid was hanging around Fort Sumner may have had to do with the suspicion that he was enamored of Paulita Maxwell, the teenaged sister of rancher Pete Maxwell. It was rumored that Paulita was pregnant with Billy the Kid's child. This has never been verified, and neither have other rumors that the Kid fathered children with Abrana Garcia as well as with Nasaria Yerby.

While finally building some momentum toward pursuing the escaped fugitive, Garrett took credit for the long-delayed inertia and stated that he approached John Poe and Thomas McKinney, both of whom were in Lincoln on business, to accompany him to Fort Sumner in search of the Kid. Poe pointed out in his book that Garrett was mistaken, that McKinney was not in Lincoln. Poe claimed that he had to talk Garrett into going to Fort Sumner and that "the following day we went to Roswell, where we found McKinney." In investigating the written accounts provided by both Garrett and Poe, it has grown burdensome trying to keep up with the obvious misstatements, lies, and contradictions, mostly those of Garrett.

It is not unusual for law enforcement officers to have somewhat different versions of an event. Garrett, however, sometimes didn't even agree with himself. In *The Authentic Life* he wrote that he, Poe, and McKinney "went to Roswell and started up the Rio Pecos from there on the night of July 10." In a letter to the New Mexico governor dated July 15, however, Garrett said: "on Monday July 11, I left home, taking with me John W. Poe and T. K. McKinney."

On the evening of July 13, the three men set up camp at the mouth of Taiban Arroyo five miles south of Fort Sumner. The next morning Poe, who was not known in the community, agreed to ride into town to see what he could find out.

Around ten a.m. Poe found himself moving about the settlement trying to learn whether or not the Kid was there. As one of only a half-dozen Anglos in the area, Poe stood out among the natives. His questions were met with suspicion, answers were vague and misleading, and he learned little. Following his visit to Fort Sumner, Poe rode seven miles north of town to the ranch of Milnor Rudolph near the small community of Sunnyside. Rudolph told Poe that he had heard the Kid was in Fort Sumner but that he did not believe it. Rudolph said that the Kid was too smart to be hanging about the place when he knew lawmen were searching for him and there was a reward for his capture or killing.

When Poe rendezvoused with Garrett and McKinney that evening at the prearranged location of Punta de la Glorieta, four miles north of Fort Sumner, he related his experience to the sheriff. Garrett was reluctant to continue the search, and by extension he was likely reluctant to encounter the Kid, but Poe's strong conviction that the Kid was nearby, along with his encouragement, caused the sheriff to agree to pursue the original objective. It was decided that they would maintain a watch on the home of Celsa Gutierrez, another of the Kid's girlfriends. Celsa lived with her husband in a small apartment that was once part of the post quartermaster's store.

Garrett decided to ride into the tiny community and visit with Pete Maxwell. If anyone knew the whereabouts of the Kid, reasoned the sheriff, it would be the rancher. According to Garrett, the three lawmen had ridden to a point close to Maxwell's residence when they came upon a campsite occupied by a man named Jacobs. Here they unsaddled, shared some coffee, and proceeded on foot to a nearby orchard.

In his book Garrett stated that the orchard ran from the campsite "down to a row of old buildings . . . not more than sixty yards from Maxwell's house." As Garrett, Poe, and McKinney approached the houses, Garrett said, they "heard the sound of voices conversing in Spanish," though they were too far away to hear words distinctly. As they watched from hiding, "a man rose from the ground, in full view, but too far away to recognize. He wore a broad-brimmed hat, a dark vest and pants, and was in his shirt sleeves." This man, claimed Garrett, was Billy the Kid, even though he previously stated he was "too far away to recognize."

A few lines later, however, Garrett again wrote, "The Kid by me unrecognized." Did Garrett recognize the Kid or not? Once more he contradicts himself. It is easy for one to suspect that Garrett, whose veracity by this time is easily questioned, was making an attempt to portray the danger as being greater than it actually was. Could it be that the incident never happened? Could it be that Garrett made it up? It would seem so.

Garrett based his "recognition" on the mode of apparel worn by the subject, but the young man who entered Maxwell's bedroom a short time later, a man Garrett identified as Billy the Kid with no hesitation, was clothed in completely different garb. Following this event, the three lawmen continued on toward Maxwell's house.

These two contentions by Garrett carry with them no logic or reason whatsoever. Experience and analysis provide for no other conclusion than that they could not have happened the way he described them, if, in fact, they happened at all.

John Poe's version of what took place differed markedly from Garrett's. Poe never mentioned Jacobs or pausing at a campsite for coffee. Poe further stated that they entered the peach orchard and stationed themselves in the "gloom of the shadow of the peach trees." From this point they watched the buildings for two hours. Finally, according to Poe, Garrett stated that he felt like they weren't accomplishing anything and proposed they leave town.

In Poe's account there is no mention of hearing voices or of observing the man Garrett claimed was Billy the Kid, or anyone else, for that matter. The latter would seem to be an important point, if indeed it ever happened. It is likely that Garrett fabricated the entire episode. Poe also wrote that he suggested that instead of leaving town they go to Maxwell's residence and determine what sort of pertinent information the rancher might have about the Kid's whereabouts. Here we have two widely varying versions of the same event by two men who claimed to have experienced it together.

Regardless of the conflicting and contradictory versions of the journey to and arrival at Fort Sumner, the three lawmen, at long last, were apparently confident that Billy the Kid was nearby and, if the fates were with them, would be encountered and either captured or killed.

Chapter Seventeen

SHOOTING AT FORT SUMNER

Pat Garrett claimed that on the night of July 14, 1881, he finally caught up with and killed the outlaw Billy the Kid. Leading deputies John Poe and Kip McKinney, the sheriff, instead of following the main road, took an alternate path and arrived at Maxwell's house from the opposite direction. The one-story structure had a porch extending across the front on the northeast side. After leaving the orchard, Garrett, Poe, and McKinney traveled a southeastern-oriented path that passed to the rear of Maxwell's house, turned northeasterly along the side of the structure, and arrived at the porch. The premises were enclosed by a "paling fence, one side of which ran parallel to and along the edge of the street up to and across the end of the porch to the corner of the building." Leaving Poe and McKinney "at the end of the porch, about twenty feet from the door of Pete's room," Garrett wrote, he "stepped onto the porch and entered Maxwell's room through the open door left open on account of the extremely warm weather." Poe stated that he "sat on the edge of the porch in the small open gateway leading from the street onto the porch" while McKinney squatted on the outside of the fence.

It is worth noting here that Poe had never seen Billy the Kid, or Pete Maxwell, for that matter. Some claim that McKinney had never seen the Kid either, though others maintain that the two had known one another, if only slightly.

After entering Maxwell's room and finding the rancher in bed, Garrett stated that he walked to the head of it and sat down on it near the pillow and next to the rancher. Maxwell told the sheriff that the Kid had been around but that he didn't know whether or not he had departed.

Thirty seconds after Garrett entered Maxwell's room, Poe stated that he spotted a "man approaching me on the inside of and along the fence, some forty or fifty steps away." The man, said Poe, was bareheaded, wore only socks on his feet, and was fastening his trousers as he approached at a brisk pace. Poe initially thought the newcomer was Maxwell or some guest who was staying at the residence. According to Poe, the man was an arm's length away before he saw the deputy.

On spotting Poe, who was still seated, the newcomer allegedly pointed his six-shooter at the deputy, jumped onto the porch, and asked, *"Quien es?"* ("Who is it?") Before he could answer, Poe claims, the man backed away from him toward the door of Maxwell's room.

McKinney, who was seated, rose to his feet. As he did so, one of his spurs caught under the porch boards and he nearly fell. The newcomer laughed at this and then repeated, *"Quien es?"* several times. Poe then stood up and took a step toward the newcomer, telling him not to be alarmed. With another step forward from Poe, the man, according to the deputy's account, "backed up into the doorway of Maxwell's room."

At this point, according to Poe, the man "halted for a moment, his body concealed by the thick adobe wall at the side of the doorway, from whence he put his head and asked in Spanish for the fourth or fifth time, *"Quien es?"* Poe was within a few feet of the man when he disappeared into the room.

In contrast with Poe's description of the arrival of the man, Garrett claimed the Kid "sprang quickly into the door, looking back" and calling out *"Quien es?"* twice.

When no one replied, wrote Garrett, the man entered the room. Garrett said the newcomer held a revolver in his right hand and a butcher knife in his left. Poe had made no mention of a knife.

Garrett:

> *The Kid came towards me. Before he reached the bed, I whispered, "Who is it, Pete?" but received no reply. . . . The intruder came close to me, leaned both hands on the bed, his right hand almost touching my knee, and asked in a low tone: "Who are they, Pete?" At that same instant Maxwell whispered to me, "That's him!" Simultaneously the Kid must have seen or felt the presence of a third person at the head of the bed. He raised quickly his pistol, a self cocker, within a foot of my breast. Retreating rapidly across the room he cried:* "Quien es? Quien es?" *All this occurred in a moment. Quickly as possible I drew my revolver and fired, threw my body aside, and fired again. The second shot was useless: The Kid fell dead.*

Garrett stated that Maxwell dove over the foot of the bed, dragging the bedclothes with him. "I went to the door," said the sheriff, "and met Poe and McKinney there." Poe wrote that Garrett "came out, brushing against me as he passed." Maxwell then ran out of the room. Surprised, Poe and McKinney pointed their handguns at him, and Maxwell cried, "Don't shoot! Don't shoot!"

Poe wrote that Garrett leaned against the wall at the side of the door and said, "That was the Kid that came in there onto me, and I think I have got him." Poe replied, "Pat, the Kid would not come to this place; you have shot the wrong man." Upon this statement Garrett appeared to be in doubt himself, but then he recovered and said he was confident that the man he shot was Billy the Kid.

At this point, according to Garrett's narrative, the three lawmen entered the room, examined the body, and determined that the "ball had struck [the victim] just above the heart, and must have cut through the ventricles." Garrett claimed that he fired two shots, but stated that Poe and McKinney insisted three shots were fired. Garrett told them that the Kid "had fired one shot, between my two." Garrett said Maxwell supported this statement. John Poe wrote that Garrett's second shot struck the headboard of Maxwell's bed.

A few minutes after the shooting, according to John Poe, "quite a number of the native people had gathered around, some of them bewailing the death of their friend, while several women pleaded for permission to take charge of the body, which we allowed them to do." Poe wrote that the body was carried "across the yard to a carpenter shop where it was laid out on a workbench, the women placing their lighted candles around it." There the body of the man shot by Pat Garrett was prepared for burial.

Poe wrote that "we spent the remainder of the night on the Maxwell premises, keeping constantly on our guard, as we were expecting to be attacked by the friends of the dead man." Steve Sederwall hastens to point out that the body of the man Garrett identified as the most wanted man in the territory, an escaped fugitive, a body that they were required to take charge of, had been taken away from them and carried across the street to a carpenter's shop while the three lawmen cowered in Maxwell's house. How was this allowed to happen? Garrett's leadership from the beginning of the journey to Maxwell's ranch certainly warranted criticism, and it must also be questioned here.

Chapter Eighteen

DISCREPANCIES

It remains troubling that since the shooting at Pete Maxwell's house on July 14, 1881, researchers never noted the obvious and glaring discrepancies in the written accounts of Pat Garrett and John Poe, as well as the improbabilities of what the two lawmen claimed took place. Leon Metz, author and Garrett apologist, insisted that the two accounts support one another, but even a cursory reading of these written and published descriptions of what occurred that day reveals numerous and obvious contradictions, inconsistencies, and disparities. Close examination of both accounts suggests that neither man was telling the truth.

An efficient way to analyze what happened at Fort Sumner would be to break the incident down into five main parts: the arrival of the players at Maxwell's room, the shooting, the post-shooting activities including the removal of the body, the inquests, and the burial.

Statements about the arrival of the various players at what would become a crime scene are fraught with problems, discrepancies, and misconceptions. Extant photographs of Maxwell's house show a peaked roof with dormers. The roof and additions, however, came well after July 14, 1881. On that night the structure was a simple one-story building originally constructed and used by the United States Army. Poe described it as a "very long, one story adobe, standing end to and flush with the street, having a porch on the south side."

After pointing out the location of Maxwell's room in the southwest corner of the building to his deputies, Garrett said, he "stepped onto the porch and entered Maxwell's room through the open door." This statement is inaccurate. According to a floor plan of the building obtained from the National Archives, the door to Maxwell's room could only be entered from a hallway. To reach the room from the porch, Garrett would have had to enter the outside door, walk ten feet down the hallway, and then turn left to pass through the bedroom door. Both Garrett and Poe left this important detail out of their accounts, a detail that was obvious and hard to miss if the two lawmen were telling the truth.

Both Garrett and Poe wrote that the three lawmen entered Maxwell's room after the shooting to examine the body. If Poe did so, then he would have known that the room could only have been reached after passing three or four steps down a hallway, a detail he omitted when he recreated the scene in his book. The more one examines Poe's narrative and all of its inconsistencies, the more one begins to wonder if that deputy was actually present in Fort Sumner. There exists some evidence for such a suspicion. A man named Bundy Avants met Pete Maxwell years after the shooting in Fort Sumner. In an article titled "The Bundy Avants Story" published in 1978, Avants talked about a conversation he had with the rancher regarding the shooting of Billy the Kid by Pat Garrett. Maxwell mentioned two things of note: It was *not* Billy the Kid who was shot and killed by Garrett, and Deputy John Poe was *not* present.

Maxwell also told Avants that Garrett was "pretty well shook up, as he didn't want it said that he had killed the wrong man." The man who was killed, said Maxwell, was a Mexican. Maxwell had promised Garrett he would keep quiet about the mistake.

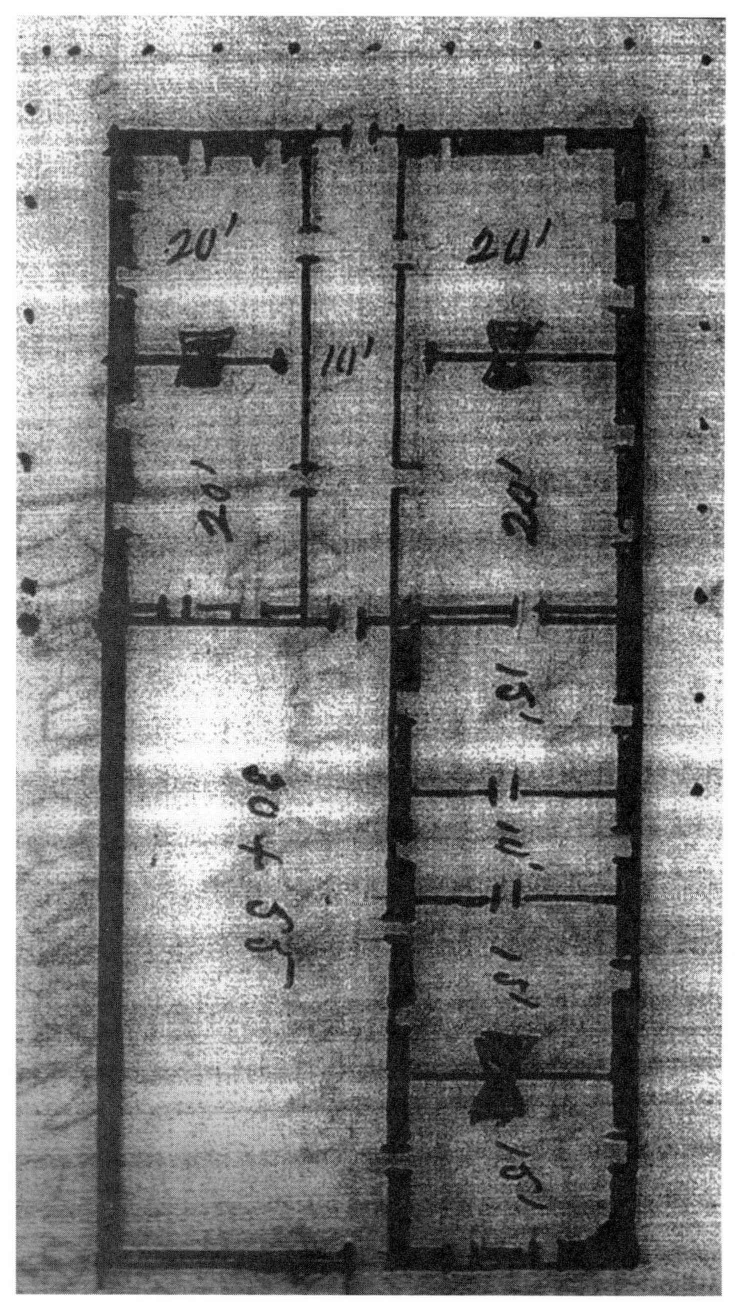

Floor plan of the Maxwell house

NATIONAL ARCHIVES

Then there is the business about the open door. July 14 in Fort Sumner, New Mexico—located on the plains in the eastern part of the state, altitude 4,032 feet, latitude just over 34 degrees N—can reasonably be assumed to be warm. In the days before air conditioning, windows were opened to allow a breeze to enter a room, but never a door. The Maxwell house was oriented northeast-southwest. Maxwell's room, according to the floor plan, had four windows, two on the northwest side and two on the southwest side. It is assumed that at least one and probably all of them were open. The door, however, was closed.

Common and plentiful members of the fauna found in this part of the desert southwest include skunks and rattlesnakes. Skunks are nocturnal creatures and are adept at finding their way under and into buildings, including barns, chicken coops, tack sheds, and houses. Skunks will boldly walk into a house through an open door. Skunks carry rabies. In 1881 residents who encountered skunks in close proximity had to deal with this serious threat as well as the potential for the animals to emit their foul and tenacious odor. No one under any circumstance ever left their bedroom door open at night in Fort Sumner in July. Having said that, it is entirely possible that Maxwell left his interior bedroom door open, but the door that provided entrance to the building would have been closed. The descriptions offered by Garrett and Poe were inconsistent with the truth.

So what exactly did Garrett do? From his published account it is impossible to tell with any degree of certainty.

Before entering Maxwell's room, Garrett told Poe and McKinney, "You fellows wait here while I go in and talk with him." To any professional lawman, according to Steve Sederwall, this does not ring true. Garrett was searching for the most dangerous outlaw in New Mexico, the most wanted man in the territory, a man he knew was armed, a man already sentenced to hang for the killing of Sheriff William Brady, a fearless outlaw who had already killed two of his deputies and had demonstrated that he would not go to the gallows easily. Garrett had no idea what awaited him inside the building or in Maxwell's room, yet he left his armed deputies, his "backup" in modern cop parlance, behind. If what Garrett says was true, he would be one of the most incompetent lawmen to ever wear a badge.

After entering Maxwell's room, twenty feet by twenty feet, Garrett "walked to the head of the bed and sat down on it" and began a conversation with the rancher. A few minutes later a man approached the building from the road and spotted the two deputies waiting outside. He was described as walking in his stockinged feet and buttoning his pants. According to both Garrett and Poe, the newcomer carried a six-shooter in one hand and a butcher knife in the left. He was not wearing a pistol belt.

Until Steve Sederwall undertook an investigation of these accounts, no one had ever proposed serious and intelligent questions directed toward what might have actually happened. An obvious one would be: If the man was carrying a handgun and a knife, how could he be buttoning his pants, a task that requires both hands?

And what about the stockinged feet? In 1881 most cowhands (and outlaws) owned one or two pairs of socks, if any. Socks were sometimes hard to come by, so the owner would try to make them last. The roads and pathways in Fort Sumner were composed of dirt and gravel, a surface that would be hard on bare feet and socks. Further, the ground would have had then, as now, a carpet of gravel, rocks, and sand burrs that stick to cloth and have the ability to puncture flesh. In addition to rocks and sand burrs, the grounds at night would be populated by the aforementioned skunks and rattlesnakes, as well as scorpions, poisonous centipedes, and horse manure. It strains logic to believe that a person would go about on foot at night in a Fort Sumner street wearing only socks. If the newcomer thought far enough ahead to carry a handgun in anticipation of trouble, would it not stand to reason that he would also take an extra few seconds to tug on his boots?

Poe wrote: "Upon his seeing me, [the newcomer] covered me with his six-shooter as quick as lightning, sprang onto the porch, calling out in Spanish, '*Quien es?*' (Who is it?)—at the same time backing toward the door through which Garrett only a few seconds before had passed." Poe said he walked toward the man "trying to reassure him," then said the man backed into the shadows, taking cover behind the thick adobe. A moment later the man popped his head out from his hiding place and "asked in Spanish for the fourth or fifth time who I was."

Poe did not speak Spanish. When Poe said he walked toward the man trying to reassure him, it can be assumed that he spoke English. The Kid, who was bilingual, would at that point have likely responded to him in English. Logic leaves us with only two options: Either this was not Billy the Kid who walked up to the lawmen or this incident did not happen.

Poe's statements are in error. Given the layout of the Maxwell residence, the newcomer, while talking with Poe, could only have backed into the doorway that opened into the main hallway of the building.

There are two additional puzzling elements to this sequence as described by Poe. First, all of this conversation was taking place within twenty feet of an open window to Pete Maxwell's bedroom. Outside of the building there were two deputies confronting an armed stranger and exchanging words, yet we are asked to believe that neither Maxwell nor Garrett heard any of this. This is simply too much to require of the curious and intelligent reader. Second, we are also asked to believe that the two deputies, having watched their sheriff enter the same doorway only moments before, would allow an armed man they did not know to simply walk away from them and into Maxwell's room without shouting a warning, without going in after him with weapons raised. This, of course, is preposterous.

More importantly, if the man who approached Maxwell's room that night was the Kid, living on the run, sentenced to hang, and hiding out because of the posted reward for his capture or death, he would hardly have paused long enough to ask Poe and McKinney a question. The Kid had been informed that a posse was on his trail, and several citizens of Fort Sumner had alerted him to the presence of Garrett. The Kid would surely have been more careful than to have simply blundered up to Maxwell's house on a night that he knew there were lawmen looking for him. To believe otherwise defies common sense. Even Poe told Garrett, "The Kid would not come to this place."

The fugitive, having already killed Olinger and Bell, would most likely have avoided any confrontation. If confrontation were inevitable, the Kid would have been more inclined to shoot the two deputies than to pause long enough to ask them questions. According to Poe, there was a full moon—actually eighty-seven percent of full—and light enough for anyone to see that the two men hanging around outside of Maxwell's bedroom were not Fort Sumner residents. The presence of strangers in the area was certainly enough to arouse the suspicion of a man wanted for killing law enforcement officers, a man who knew he was being pursued, unless, of course, the man who went to Maxwell's room was not Billy the Kid.

Given the evidence provided by Garrett and Poe, given a thorough deconstruction, analysis, and reconstruction, it is clear that this incident as the two lawmen described it never took place and that both the sheriff and his deputy manufactured their versions of the story.

As Garrett was seated on Maxwell's bed and deep in conversation with the rancher, he claimed, "A man sprang quickly into the door." The man was bareheaded, in his "stocking-feet, and held a revolver in his right hand and a butcher knife in his left." Garrett said that "the intruder came close to me, leaned both hands on the bed, his right hand almost touching my knee, and asked in a low tone: 'Who are they, Pete?'"

Garrett's statement begs a challenge. The intruder is so close that his right hand almost touches the sheriff's knee, yet the man cannot see the sheriff. According to Garrett's published account, from more than ten feet away he insisted he saw the man carrying a revolver and a knife. He also claimed that he could even identify the type of weapon the intruder was carrying—"a self cocker." Why is it that one man was able to see details in this dark room and the other was not?

After the newcomer asked Maxwell the question, Garrett stated that the rancher whispered, "That's him!"

The account Garrett presented in his book differs from what he reported to the governor in his letter of July 15, a portion of which was quoted in the previous chapter. In his letter Garrett stated that he believed the Kid had seen him enter Maxwell's bedroom, or had been informed that the sheriff was there, and that the Kid came "armed with pistol and knife expressly to kill me."

If what Garrett wrote had any element of truth to it, that the Kid arrived at Maxwell's room "expressly" to kill him, why then would the Kid, who was aware that Garrett and his deputies were searching for him and would have been on the alert for the sheriff or any other lawmen, stumble into the dark bedroom asking Maxwell who was outside? Garrett, in fact, contradicts himself. Did Garrett lie about the encounter with the intruder in the bedroom or about the notion that the Kid arrived to kill him? Or did he lie about both?

The business about the intruder carrying both a handgun and a butcher knife has been questioned. Did the man Garrett claimed to be the Kid carry a gun at all? In *Violence in Lincoln County* (University of New Mexico Press, 1957), author William H. Keleher wrote that the person who walked into Maxwell's bedroom had only a knife. Author Robert M. Utley wrote that a "belief persists that Billy was armed only with a butcher knife" and that "Garrett and Poe had reason to want the world to believe that Billy carried a pistol." In *History of the Lincoln County War* (University of Arizona Press, 1968), Maurice G. Fulton stated that the man carried only a butcher knife. Former New Mexico governor Miguel Otero, who interviewed Fort Sumner residents Francisco Lobato, Jesus Silva, and Deluvina Maxwell, learned that the man shot by Garrett did not have a pistol in his possession when he was killed.

Was a pistol placed in the right hand of the dead man after the shooting to make it appear that he was armed? Garrett, who had high political ambitions, must have realized that shooting an unarmed man would not look good. If indeed a pistol were provided, a so-called drop weapon, whoever did so made a mistake and gave the dead man a gun Billy the Kid was never known to use.

There is more. There is no agreement on whether two shots were fired or three, and there is disagreement on whether the body of the slain man was inside or outside the room. Author Frederick Nolan contends that *The Authentic Life* was written to make Garrett look good, that it was necessary to "exaggerate the Kid's recklessness, his gun fighting skills, his murderous nature," all designed to "present Garrett as a courageous lawman."

Odelia Bernice Finley Johnson, daughter of Pete Maxwell, once related an account by Deluvina Maxwell, who was one of Pete Maxwell's employees. Deluvina Maxwell's story conflicts with the positions taken by Garrett and Poe. According to Johnson, Garrett and the two deputies were afraid to enter the room after the shooting, believing that the stranger was only wounded and lying in wait for them. After roundly cursing Garrett, Deluvina grabbed a candle and walked into the bedroom—perhaps the first to do so—to render aid to the victim.

Garrett wrote that, as he sat on Maxwell's bed, he drew his "revolver and fired, threw my body aside, and fired again." This statement represents additional troubling inconsistencies. Given the proximity of Maxwell's open bedroom window to the front porch, the two men seated on the bed were likely no more than twenty feet away from where Poe, McKinney, and the newcomer were speaking outside the open window. Garrett must have heard them, for he even said, "McKinney, who was seated, rose to his feet. As he did so, one of his spurs caught under the porch and he nearly fell." The newcomer laughed at this and then said *"Quien es?"* several times. Poe then stepped up and told the newcomer not to be alarmed. It is inconceivable that Garrett could detect the sound of McKinney stumbling but hear nothing of the nearby conversation between the newcomer and Poe. There exist far too many inconsistencies for comfort. It is inconceivable that Garrett could not have heard the three men talking as well as the commotion, however slight, of McKinney tripping, his spurs surely jingling as he did so. Hearing the arrival of the newcomer, Garrett, suspecting Billy the Kid was in the neighborhood and wanting to kill him, would not have waited for the newcomer to enter the room, place his hands on the bed, and ask Maxwell a question before pulling his revolver. An experienced lawman would never allow such a thing to happen. Garrett lied about this episode.

Garrett also lied when he wrote that he drew his revolver and fired, "threw my body aside, and fired again." In order for this statement to be true, Garrett, in throwing his body aside, would have had to make a giant leap from the bed to the opposite side of the room, a distance of no less than fifteen feet, for his second bullet perforated the washstand at an angle that indicated he was on his knees in the far corner of the room when he fired (see the crime scene investigation of Maxwell's bedroom furniture at the end of this chapter).

Garrett wrote that he, Poe, and McKinney "searched long and faithfully—found both my bullet marks and none other." Where could the deputies have found the bullet marks? If Garrett had found the bullet holes in the washstand, he surely would not have admitted that the bullet came from his gun, for it proved that his initial explanation of what happened was untrue. And where was the second "mark"? Did Garrett suggest the bullet that struck the newcomer in the chest passed through his body and punctured the wall behind him?

It is important to analyze Garrett's shooting of the newcomer and subsequent behavior in greater detail. One such analysis was provided from the standpoint of an expert experienced with such things. Steve Sederwall contacted David A. Brewer, a Homeland Security and senior law enforcement specialist for the Federal Law Enforcement Training Center in Artesia, New Mexico, a man well qualified to assess such behavior.

According to Brewer, stressful situations such as a shooting generate increases in heart rates to levels exceeding 140 beats per minute. In response, the brain tells the body to reduce blood flow to the fine motor skills muscles and increase it to the large motor skills muscles. This enables the individual to engage the "fight or flight" mode.

In many cases other involuntary responses occur, including perceptual narrowing, loss of peripheral vision, images appearing in black and white, auditory occlusion, involuntary tracking of threats, increased blood pressure, and loss of one's ability to think clearly.

A second area of research indicates that the body reacts to certain stimuli that can cause the body to flinch or react involuntarily. The three common stimuli are fear or sudden surprise, push-pull reflex, and imbalance. An example of fear or sudden surprise reflex would be a police officer pursuing a suspect in a dark building and having the suspect suddenly jump out from a hiding place, causing a startle effect. If the officer had his weapon in single-action mode (cocked hammer), he would more than likely discharge his weapon by jerking the trigger out of a reflex action.

An example of imbalance occurs when a police officer is pursuing a suspect with his weapon in hand and suddenly loses balance. A reflex action occurs in the gun hand that increases the pressure on the trigger finger, thus causing the accidental discharge of the weapon.

It is clear that Brewer's descriptions fit the sequence of events in which Pat Garrett was involved. Garrett, who was already on edge as a result of attempting to arrest or kill the outlaw Billy the Kid in a dark room around midnight at one of the Kid's known haunts, a man he clearly feared, was in a stressful situation. Garrett was then startled by the newcomer entering Maxwell's bedroom, which further caused an increase in heart rate and blood pressure, thus engaging the fight-or-flight mode.

Garrett responded and reacted to the newcomer as a result of the fear Brewer described, fear that caused the lawman to raise his revolver and shoot the intruder, a reflex action. Garrett then stated that he "threw my body aside, and fired again." Garrett not only threw his body aside but also scrambled around in a desperate attempt to flee from the room. From a panicked, and unbalanced, position on the floor, the frightened sheriff fired his second shot. Because he was still blinded by the flash of the first shot and unable to perceive clearly where he was in the room or what he was shooting at, his second bullet struck the washstand.

Given the evidence available for determining what happened in Maxwell's bedroom that night, it is obvious that there is no consensus and little to support the notion that Garrett was telling the truth about anything. Garrett's published words, in fact, bear the unmistakable mark of fabrication.

Leon Metz has written that almost "from the moment that Garrett's pistol cracked in Pete Maxwell's bedroom and Billy toppled to the floor, controversy has surrounded the killing." And in a surprise statement, on being confronted with the ponderous evidence of contradiction and lying, Metz even acknowledged that "there is enough evidence, indeed, to make one wonder whether Garrett actually killed [Billy the Kid] at all." According to writer Frederick Nolan, Garrett's "recital of circumstances surrounding the Kid's death on the night of July 14, 1881, may have been the biggest lie of all." Author Jon Tuska in his book *Billy the Kid: A Handbook* refers to this entire sequence as a Garrett fantasy.

In his letter to the territorial governor, written on July 15, wherein he informed him of the shooting, Garrett stated, "It was my desire to have been able to take him alive, but his coming upon me so suddenly and unexpectedly led me to believe that he had seen me enter the room, or had been informed by some one of the fact, and that he came there armed with pistol and knife expressly to kill me if he could." More on this statement later.

But Deputy Poe offered a different version. He stated that the darkness within the room was such "that we were unable to see what the conditions were on the inside or what the result of the shooting had been." Following what he referred to as "forceful persuasion," Poe stated that he convinced Maxwell to bring a tallow candle. Maxwell placed the candle on the windowsill outside the room, the dim light being just enough to allow them to see a man lying stretched out on his back and clearly dead. Convinced that the man on the floor was no longer a threat, only then did the three lawmen dare to enter the room.

Given that Poe claimed to have entered the room in which the newcomer was shot and killed, he would have had to have passed through the outside doorway, walked three to four steps down the hall, and then passed through a second doorway into the rancher's room. Yet in his book Poe referred to only one doorway. His description of what happened could not possibly have happened that way. Poe was describing a situation that could not have occurred.

While Poe stated that the dead man was lying on his back, Jesus Silva told Miguel Antonio Otero in *The Real Billy the Kid: With New Light on the Lincoln County War* that when he entered Maxwell's bedroom moments after the shooting, the dead man was "stretched out, face down." Silva claimed that after entering the room "we turned him over." Did Silva enter the room before the lawmen?

Poe relates that a short time after the shooting, a number of Fort Sumner residents gathered, took possession of the body, and transported it a short distance to a carpenter shop, where they laid it out on a workbench and prepared it for burial. Since the shooting occurred, according to all of the experts, just after midnight, it can be assumed that the body was removed from the crime scene at around one a.m.

Published history also tells us that a coroner's jury was held to conduct an inquest later that same morning, and shortly thereafter the body was buried. According to some, Milnor Rudolph of Sunnyside was summoned by Garrett to serve as foreman of the coroner's jury. According to author Robert Utley, Alejandro Segura, the Fort Sumner justice of the peace, sent for Rudolph. Regardless of who sent for Rudolph, it can logically be assumed that it was around one a.m. that Garrett selected someone to locate and saddle and bridle a horse and set out for Sunnyside to summon Rudolph.

Any experienced horseman would figure that it would take about thirty minutes to retrieve a horse from a stable and saddle and bridle it, thus providing a generous estimate of one thirty a.m. when the messenger rode out of Fort Sumner. It was night, and even with a nearly full moon, a rider would be traveling slower than during the day. Since an average speed for a walking horse is under four miles per hour, it would take approximately two hours to reach Rudolph's house, the rider arriving at around three thirty a.m.

Milnor was fifty-five years of age and in relatively good health. Allot him a generous thirty minutes to awaken and respond to the knock on his door, listen to and process the message, get dressed, and saddle his horse or ready his wagon. By four a.m. he was on his way to Fort Sumner. It was still dark, and Rudolph took two hours to make the trip and meet Garrett at six a.m. This timeline fits Garrett's statement that the inquest was held "the following morning."

The subsequent coroner's report states that the "jury convened at the home of Luz B. Maxwell and proceeded to a room in the said house where they found the body of William Bonney alias 'Kid.'" This is another tell missed by the historians. If the body was, as Poe stated, taken to a carpenter's workshop and was being prepared for burial, how is it that Rudolph found the dead man back on the floor of Maxwell's room? It is improbable that the body was reclaimed from the carpenter shop and repositioned on the floor.

With respect to the prevailing legend, there is something clearly wrong here. Either Poe was not telling the truth or the jury report was a lie.

It gets more confusing. Justice Segura instructed Rudolph to assemble a coroner's jury and serve as foreman. The inquest was conducted by Segura. Rudolph selected five men, who listened to Garrett recount the events of the previous evening. Rudolph wrote out the report, and it was signed by him and the five jurors. Some of the jurors could not write and made their mark. The report read in part:

> *William Bonney was killed by a shot in the left breast, in the region of the heart, fired from a pistol in the hand of Patrick F. Garrett, and our verdict is that the act of the said Garrett was justifiable homicide, and we are unanimous in the opinion that the gratitude of the whole community is due to the said Garrett for his act and that he deserves to be rewarded.*

According to Steve Sederwall, the part of this statement that reads "the gratitude of the whole community is due to . . ." represents another tell, one that strongly suggests that this statement was concocted to provide praise for Garrett, and likely dictated by Garrett himself. Remember that Fort Sumner residents were almost entirely in sympathy with their friend, Billy the Kid. Poe had written that after the body had been taken away the three lawmen locked themselves in Maxwell's bedroom "constantly on guard as we were expecting to be attacked." Poe's description does not make it sound that the lawmen, Garrett in particular, deserved or were awarded "the gratitude of the whole community." The community was, in fact, anything but grateful.

For reasons never explained, this report was never entered into the official records of San Miguel County. In addition, Justice Segura never made an entry regarding the report in his own books. Even more perplexing and stunning is that the Rudolph report was apparently the second coroner's report made that day; the first was made a short time after the shooting.

Like the shooting, the inquest of the man Garrett claimed was Billy the Kid has been shrouded in confusion and mystery. In his book *I Buried Billy*, A. P. Anaya stated that the report Garrett presented is "neither the form or the writing" of the original report. Anaya, a former member of the New Mexico state legislature, said during an interview with George Fitzpatrick of *New Mexico* magazine that he and a friend "were called as members of the coroner's jury the night the Kid was killed, and that this jury wrote out a verdict stating simply that the Kid had come to his death as a result of a wound from a gun at the hands of Pat Garrett, officer." Whether the members of this jury actually saw the body of the slain man was never made clear.

Anaya said this verdict was lost and that Garrett and Manuel Abreau wrote a second one, a "more flowery one for filing." New signatures other than those of Anaya and those who witnessed the first report appeared on the second one. Anaya also stated that Milnor Rudolph was not a member of the original jury. Anaya said the second report was a fake, and that two of the men listed on Garrett's report as being members of the coroner's jury did not even live in Fort Sumner. In truth, Milnor Rudolph did not live in Fort Sumner.

The speed with which the inquest was handled was peculiar and suspect. According to writer Frank Richard Prassell in *The Great American Outlaw*, "Lawmen of the era normally went to considerable effort to verify the deaths of fugitives for two good reasons: To foreclose a later charge of killing an innocent party and to facilitate the collection of rewards."

The sequence of events relating to the two inquests is, to say the least, unusual, and the contradictions and inconsistencies invite suspicion, particularly of the individual overseeing the proceedings—Sheriff Pat Garrett.

According to William A. Keleher, author of *Violence in Lincoln County*, the second coroner's report was written in Spanish and attached to a cover letter written by Garrett. Keleher claimed that he saw a copy of the document in the Office of the Commissioner of Public Lands in Santa Fe. (Long believed to have been lost, this report, written in Spanish, was recently located in the possession of a New Mexico resident.) According to the report, said Keleher, the words spoken by the man who entered Maxwell's bedroom were in English, not Spanish, as Garrett and Poe claimed. Additionally, either some of the signers of the second report misspelled their own names or Rudolph misspelled them. According to E. B. Mann in his book *Guns and Gunfighters*, only three witnesses identified the body, and one of them later stated that it was *not* Billy the Kid who was killed but another person.

The possibility exists that Garrett was aware of killing an innocent man, a man who stumbled into Maxwell's bedroom who was not Billy the Kid, and wanted the process to move quickly so that the victim could be buried before the mistake was discovered. There is a belief among a number of researchers that Pat Garrett himself dictated the second coroner's report because he was unsatisfied with the findings of the first.

It has become obvious that a series of inconsistencies, contradictions, half-truths, and perhaps outright lies have been detected relating to what should have been a cut-and-dried case. Something is wrong with all of this. According to Sederwall, none of what happened at Fort Sumner proceeded in a manner consistent with honest and forthright law enforcement. Somebody (or somebodies) is lying. If that is true, and all of the evidence seems to point in that direction, then the question becomes: Why are they lying? The only answer is that they did something wrong and were trying to cover it up. Believe it or not, it gets even more convoluted over the next few hours following the inquests.

On the afternoon of July 15, 1881, the man identified by Sheriff Pat Garrett as the outlaw Billy the Kid was interred in a wooden coffin at the Fort Sumner military cemetery next to the graves of Charlie Bowdre and Tom Folliard. The burial, like the sequence of events leading to the arrival at Pete Maxwell's house, the shooting, and the inquests, is not free from controversy, questions, contradictions, and criticism.

Since the shooting in Maxwell's room, barely more than twelve hours had passed before Garrett had the body of the dead man placed in the ground. The incredibly short span of time that elapsed between the shooting and the burial was astonishing and heretofore unheard of.

In addition, bear in mind that, according to Sheriff Garrett, he had just shot and killed the most wanted man in New Mexico, a notorious desperado who by this time had garnered headlines throughout much of the United States. Killing Billy the Kid would have been regarded as the most significant event of that decade, an event that would have drawn reporters and photographers from far and wide to record the event and interview the heroic sheriff. In a very short time, newspapermen and photographers from nearby

Roswell, Santa Fe, Albuquerque, Las Vegas, and Las Cruces could have arrived on the scene.

Also recall that Garrett was a politician, one who had his sights set on running for higher offices than county sheriff. The resulting publicity would have been a career-changing boon for him. Yet not only did he choose not to inform news outlets, he wasted no time at all in getting the body of the dead man into the ground. Why?

Bear in mind another fact. When a noted bad man was killed, the practice of that time was to have the corpse placed on display and photographed. This was done with Jesse James, the Dalton Gang, Bitter Creek Newcomb, Charlie Pierce, the Doolin Gang, Ned Christie, the casualties of the shooting at the OK Corral, and others. Garrett did none of this and had the body interred posthaste. It seemed as though Garrett could not get the body of his victim in the ground soon enough. And for what reason? There can only be one: Pat Garrett did something wrong, something he did not wish to be exposed. The most obvious consideration is that he shot the wrong man.

Pat Garrett, as has been clearly shown, was not beyond being duplicitous and self-serving at the expense of truth. If he had been honest, and if everything related to this killing had gone according to the law, none of the aforementioned ploys would have been necessary.

For years historians and writers have accepted, even embraced, the words of Pat Garrett and John Poe relating to the shooting at Fort Sumner. Such is apparent in the body of literature on that topic that has flowed out for public consumption over the past 130 years. The matter has been "researched" time and again, but until Steve Sederwall decided to apply his expertise to this event, it had never been thoroughly and professionally investigated. To many, Pat Garrett was a hero, the stalwart lawman who brought down a famous outlaw. To investigator Sederwall, Pat Garrett's trail is littered with lies, deceptions, and cover-ups.

The entire series of events related to the alleged shooting of the outlaw Billy the Kid by Sheriff Pat Garrett in Fort Sumner on July 14, 1881, is replete with contradiction, inconsistency, and lies. The written and published accounts of two of the principals—Garrett and Deputy John Poe—cannot be trusted, nor can the hundreds of other treatments of this episode that have been published since then because the writers simply parroted the so-called official version. Garrett and Poe purposefully got it wrong.

John Poe's manuscript on the death of the Kid, originally published in *Wide World Magazine* and coming nearly four decades after the shooting, seemed quite precise regarding Garrett's statements from that long-ago night. Was Poe's memory so keen that he remembered the sheriff's exact words? Or is it more likely that his recollections of that night were influenced by his own reading of Garrett's account? Or was John Poe even present?

And why, after disagreeing with Garrett that night on numerous matters as well as who was actually killed, did Poe finally come around to supporting the sheriff's version? The answer may lie in the fact that both men were members of the same fraternal organization, the Masons, and were committed to a fraternal bond that might have induced them to synchronize their stories. This explanation has been offered by a number of Masons.

Fort Sumner was an active crime scene location beginning on the evening of July 14, 1881, and lasting for less than twenty-four hours. Specifically, Pete Maxwell's bedroom was the focus, but the carpenter's shop where the body of the dead man was placed on the workbench held a level of importance. Five persons were involved with or were in the immediate area of the crime: Sheriff Pat Garrett, deputies John Poe and Kip McKinney, Pete Maxwell, and the man Garrett claimed was Billy the Kid. Historians have focused on these participants yet have ignored other aspects of the crime scene, mainly the furniture in Maxwell's bedroom. As opposed to the historian, the investigator feels compelled to examine such artifacts since they always have the potential for clues. Artifacts such as these are regarded as important evidence by law enforcement personnel who attempt to determine what may have taken place at a crime scene.

The workbench takes on a potential level of importance because of the possibility that it contained bloodstains from the slain intruder. Blood samples can provide DNA, and if any DNA acquired from the bench could be compared to known relatives of Billy the Kid, the resultant analysis might answer some questions.

The first question, however, is: What became of the workbench? The historical record claimed that during a severe flood of the nearby Pecos River in 1906, the Maxwell house was washed away, along with, presumably, everything in it. This event provided a challenge; Steve Sederwall determined that it was important to learn whether or not it actually happened.

Initially, the building that eventually became the Maxwell house was constructed by the US Army shortly after Fort Sumner was established on October 31, 1862. It was used as an officers' quarters. The building was constructed of adobe bricks; the two exterior doors, front and back, were made from one-and-three-quarter-inch lumber. The inside doors to the individual rooms were fashioned from three-quarter-inch lumber. The flooring was one-quarter-inch thick and the roof composed of one-inch lumber.

The military remained at Fort Sumner until June 29, 1868. In 1869 the commissioner of the General Land Office determined that the property be returned to "the body of public domain, surveyed, and thrown open to settlement." In 1870, Lucien B. Maxwell, Pete's father, offered five thousand dollars for the land and the buildings. The military agreed to sell the buildings for that sum but not the land. Subsequently, Maxwell entered into an agreement with the government to lease the property on which the abandoned buildings sat.

Public Property

AT

FORT SUMNER, NEW MEXICO,

TO BE SOLD AT

LAS VEGAS, NEW MEXICO,

ON MONDAY, JUNE 13th, 1870,

in accordance with advertisement of May 12, 1870, as follows:

7 Buildings, [Adobes,] Officers Quarters, 5 rooms each,

6 Buildings, (Adobe,) Soldiers Quarters, Capacity 100 men each,
1 " " Hospital, Capacity 24 Beds,
3 " " Stables, " 100 Horses each,
4 " " Storehouses, size 175x36 feet each,
2 " (Wood,) Grain Houses, large,
1 " (Adobe,) Bake House, "
1 " " Coal House, "
3 Rooms, (Adobe,) used for Guard and Guard House,
1 Building, " 5 Rooms suitable for Officers Quarters,
2 Rooms, " (Offices,) size about 15x20 each,
1 Building, " 5 rooms, suitable for Officers Quarters,
1 " " 5 " " " " "
1 " " 7 " Laundress Quarters and Commissary issue building,
1 " " (1 room 16x16) adjacent to Bake House,
4 rooms, (Adobe,) connecting two of the Storehouses and used as Quartermaster and Commissary Offices, and quarters for clerks. Sizes are—two 20x25, and two 15x18 feet,
5 rooms, (Adobe,) connecting one side of two stables,
9 " (Small,) " " " " one stable, connected in part with 1 building, (Adobe,) about 18x22 feet, consisting of two rooms used as a Carpenter and Blacksmith shop,
1 Building, [Adobe,] 5 rooms and Bake Oven, joined to Blacksmith and Carpenter shop,
1 Slaughter House and Corral, with building on one side containing 6 rooms,

350 Cords Wood, more or less, Pinon and Cottonwood,

28,000 Shingles, Loose,

1970 Bushels Charcoal,

The sale of Buildings conveys no title to the lands upon which they are located.

Terms Cash, on Day of Sale.

A. G. ROBINSON,

Brevet Major and A. Q. M. U. S. Army,

Chief Quartermaster.

Broadside printed by the US Army to advertise the sale of Fort Sumner buildings

DAVID TURK COLLECTION.

Lucien B. Maxwell irrigated the land, raised crops, and ran a herd of cattle on it until his death on July 25, 1875. Lucien's widow, Luz, retained ownership of the buildings. The Maxwell family entered into an agreement with Manuel Brazel, a local rancher, and formed the Brazel and Maxwell Horseshoe Ranch. The management of the cattle herd fell to Lucien's son, Peter. The sheep management was turned over to Manuel Abreau, Pete's brother-in-law. Since the ranch controlled the water over most of this part of the country, it became the largest agricultural operation in the area.

Contrary to what history relates, the Fort Sumner buildings did not wash away in a flood. Sederwall learned that in 1884, three years after the shooting in Maxwell's bedroom, the army sold the land to the New England Cattle Company. Following the purchase, the new owners informed the Maxwell family that they needed to remove their buildings from the company's land. In a 1935 WPA report, J. Vernon Smith related: "The old fort was torn down for the lumber that it contained. The heavier timbers, doors, windows, and other lumber was carried away and used in other buildings. Charlie Foor, an old-time resident, helped to tear down the old Maxwell home, and is still using the floorings in his present home."

The old Charlie Foor house still stands in the town of Fort Sumner. There is a possibility that some of the floorboards contain the residue of blood from the man killed by Pat Garrett in 1881.

After the army sold the land, Pete Maxwell purchased a ranch a short distance away. All of his belongings, including the furniture in his bedroom, as well as the workbench, were moved to the new location and placed into a barn for storage.

In 1882, Manuel Brazel opted out of his partnership with the ranching enterprise, choosing to move to Colorado and look into some mining interests. On August 20, Luz Maxwell deeded the property over to her youngest daughter, Odila Abreau, Manuel Abreau's wife. During the following years a series of mortgaging and property changes and readjustments ensued. On July 13, 1900, Luz Maxwell died. Three and a half months later, on October 29, all notes were paid off.

Prior to paying off the mortgages, and because money was tight, Pete Maxwell was forced to take other work, including cooking for "wagon outfits." Pete cared little for all of the personal property that had been passed on to him by his father and turned it over to Odila. Among these items was the furniture from his bedroom in the old Maxwell house, the bed and a washstand, along with the workbench from the carpenter shop.

Stella Abreau, daughter of Odila and Manuel, was born on November 7, 1910. She was raised on the Abreau compound, and when she was thirteen years old, her mother gave her all of the items from the old fort including the bed, the washstand, and the workbench. In 1923, Stella opened a museum for tourists. On display were many of the items from the old fort.

During this time Walter Noble Burns was traveling throughout that part of New Mexico gathering material for his book *The Saga of Billy the Kid*. By chance, he stumbled onto the museum located twelve miles out of Fort Sumner. In one room he found the workbench and learned the story. When his book was published, Burns wrote to Maurice G. Fulton and told him about the workbench. Fulton was excited and in turn notified his friend the historian Robert Mullin and sent him a photograph of the bench. The photo found its way to the J. Evetts Haley Memorial Library in Midland, Texas.

In August 2003, Sederwall learned that the artifacts from Maxwell's bedroom, as well as the workbench, were in the possession of a man named Manny Miller of Albuquerque. Miller, as it turned out, was the son of Stella Abreau. After a search for a phone number in the Albuquerque phone book, the name Lucian Maxwell Miller was discovered. A call was made, and it was learned that this Miller was a brother to Manny. Manny was contacted, and arrangements were made to view the artifacts.

Stella Abreau and Maurice Fulton on the porch of the Billy the Kid Museum near Fort Sumner
J. EVETTS HALEY COLLECTION

In a chicken house located behind Manny Miller's house, Sederwall found a number of historical items under a layer of dust and cobwebs, including the workbench, the bed, and the washstand. When he asked how these pieces came to be stored in a chicken house, Manny explained that his mother's small museum had eventually closed down and all of the displayed material was locked in a barn and forgotten. Stella's sister, Billi, was married to man named Pierce. The two were planning to move to Amarillo in 1957 and decided to take the artifacts with them and open up a museum there. When Stella learned of these plans, an argument ensued. Stella was determined that the artifacts needed to remain in New Mexico. Fearing that Billi would abscond with the pieces, Stella got Manny to load them into a panel truck and move them to Albuquerque, where they had been stored for the next forty-six years.

After receiving permission from Manny, Sederwall contacted Dr. Henry Lee. The famous crime scene investigation expert was summoned to conduct analyses on the bedroom pieces. The headboard to the bed drew immediate interest. Deputy John Poe stated that the bullet from Garrett's second shot "had struck the adobe wall and rebounded against the headboard," so this artifact was examined closely, front and back. It contained nothing resembling the impact of a bullet, not even a scratch.

The workbench upon which the alleged body of Billy the Kid was laid to be prepared for burial
STEVE SEDERWALL COLLECTION

The headboard of the bed from Pete Maxwell's room
STEVE SEDERWALL COLLECTION

This begs the question: Why did Deputy Poe make such a statement? Clearly, it was not true, and amounted to nothing more than a fabrication.

The washstand, made of wood, was examined and found to have two bullet holes, one on the left side panel and one on the right side panel, one clearly an entrance hole and the other an exit hole. The inside and outside of each hole was tested for the presence of lead. Each location tested positive. The bullet Garrett

The washstand from Pete Maxwell's room
STEVE SEDERWALL COLLECTION

fired from his handgun, a Colt .44/.40, would have been lead, not copper-jacketed.

Using a laser, the angle of the bullet's path passing through the washstand was traced. The horizontal angle was 5.22 degrees, the vertical angle 4.47 degrees. The vertical angle was small, indicating that Garrett was close to the floor with his handgun nearly level with the washstand when he fired the second shot, probably in a blind panic.

The workbench was examined and tested for blood residue using the presumptive blood test reagents phenolphthalein and o-tolidine. A number of locations on both the top and underside of the workbench tested positive for blood, seven on top and ten on the underside near joints. In sufficient quantity, blood from a body, or a number of bodies over several years, placed on top of the workbench could easily have seeped through the narrow space where the planks came together and along the edges. Enough blood samples were collected to perform a DNA test. The results of the DNA test showed that the blood was from two different human beings. There is a possibility that the DNA could be separated, but such a procedure had not been undertaken at this writing.

Chapter Nineteen

POLITICS VS. TRUTH

Within minutes following the shooting in Pete Maxwell's bedroom, it was being whispered throughout Fort Sumner that the dead man was not Billy the Kid, as claimed by Pat Garrett. In a short time rumors to that effect began to spread throughout the countryside and grew stronger, more insistent, with each telling.

During the following decades a few men were linked to the identity of the outlaw Billy the Kid, a man who survived the alleged killing by Sheriff Pat Garrett. Some of these men made outright claims that they were the notorious outlaw; others were identified by acquaintances as being the outlaw. Most of these claims were easily dismissed, but two of them carried sufficient traction as to cause people to wonder about what might have actually happened in rancher Maxwell's room. Over time the number of people who grew convinced that Pat Garrett was not trustworthy and might not have killed Billy the Kid swelled.

A man who went by the name John Miller passed away in the Arizona Pioneer Home in Prescott, Arizona, on November 7, 1937. A few people—Miller himself, along with some family members and friends—made the claim that he was Billy the Kid. In an attempt to lend validation to this notion, a book was published in 1993 (*Whatever Happened to Billy the Kid?* by Helen Airy) but provided little more than anecdotal evidence. Still, the question lingered: Could John Miller have been the legendary outlaw?

Steve Sederwall's ongoing investigation of Billy the Kid and the events surrounding his life took the investigator to Miller's gravesite with the intent of gathering evidence. On May 9, 2005, an exhumation of the claimant by a forensic anthropologist and authorized by the state of Arizona yielded some interesting findings. The right scapula of Miller manifested a round hole. The anthropologist observed that it appeared to be bullet hole that had healed. If it had indeed been a bullet wound, the bullet had entered the man's upper chest and exited out his back. Was there a possibility that this could have resulted from a bullet fired from Pat Garrett's weapon? A provocative theory, but one that would require more evidence.

Miller's remains showed something else of interest—the teeth. His right front incisor was placed somewhat in front of his left front incisor, a feature that would have provided him with a dental feature not unlike that seen in the only authenticated photograph of Billy the Kid. During the examination Sederwall obtained DNA material from Miller's remains sufficient to conduct a test.

On December 27, 1950, a man named William Henry Roberts, who went by the alias Oliver L. Roberts, died of coronary occlusion in Hico, Texas. He was two days shy of his ninetieth birthday. Years earlier Roberts had been identified as Billy the Kid by acquaintances, among them a few participants in the Lincoln County War. Though Roberts initially denied he was Billy the Kid, he finally admitted the identity when confronted with evidence. Via a series of interviews conducted in the year prior to his death, Roberts provided an incredible amount of insight and information about the life and times of the Kid and of the Lincoln County War, much of it new to, and in conflict with, the historians of the day. When Roberts's revelations

William Henry Roberts, aka Billy the Kid, at eighty-eight years of age
W. C. JAMESON COLLECTION

were investigated, however, most of his claims were verified. (For details, see the author's 2005 book *Billy the Kid: Beyond the Grave.*) In the final analysis Roberts turned out to have far more credibility than Pat Garrett. In addition, though he was borderline illiterate, Roberts also possessed more knowledge about Billy the Kid and the Lincoln County War than many of the historians and writers of the time.

In 1992 the only statistically valid photo-comparison software available was requested from and provided by the US Federal Bureau of Investigation, and a study was conducted at the Laboratory for Vision Studies and the Advanced Graphics Laboratory at the University of Texas in an attempt to determine whether or not Roberts and Billy the Kid could be the same man. When the results were in, analysts Dr. Alan Bovik and Scott Acton reported, "The similarity between the facial structures of . . . Roberts and [Billy the Kid] is indeed amazing." The report stated that there was enough of a "remarkable similarity" to suggest a match. In the end, results determined that Roberts and Billy the Kid were the same man. (For the complete study, as well as additional evidence, see *Billy the Kid: Beyond the Grave.*)

The possibility of exhuming Roberts's remains from his grave in Hamilton, Texas, was explored, and plans for acquiring DNA material discussed. A request to do so was rejected by the Hamilton mayor and city council. As it turned out, the "grave" of William Henry Roberts, aka Billy the Kid, as sponsored by the city of Hamilton is prominently located within a few feet of Texas Highway 281. This grave, in fact, is a fake, a photo-op for tourists. Roberts was buried toward the rear of the cemetery in what was a paupers' section at the time of his death.

Another potential for DNA testing was the "official" remains of Billy the Kid at Fort Sumner. If Sederwall had been allowed to examine those bones and gather DNA material, he could have compared it to that found on the workbench and settled the controversy once and for all. Sederwall met with Fort Sumner mayor Raymond Lopez and explained his objectives and approach relative to his ongoing investigations directed toward Billy the Kid, the Lincoln County War, Pat Garrett, and more.

One of Sederwall's objectives was to keep Lopez and Fort Sumner officials in the information loop in case he needed to orient some investigation nearby. Lopez loved the idea, and his head was filled with visions of large flocks of tourists descending onto his town in response and spending money freely at the motels, gas stations, and cafes. Later, when Lopez intuited that Sederwall might want to dig into the alleged grave of the Kid to collect DNA, he did an about-face and grew hostile to the investigation. Did Lopez know something about this grave that Sederwall didn't?

Around this same time the writer Fred Nolan, who lived in England and regarded himself as an authority on all things Billy the Kid, wrote a letter to a local newspaper stating that Sederwall should cease his investigations. It made Sederwall wonder what Nolan was concerned about. Was he worried that Sederwall might discover a truth that was in conflict with Nolan's support of the legend? It would seem so.

During this time Sederwall also made plans to attempt to acquire DNA from the Silver City grave of Catherine Antrim, identified by some as the mother of the Kid. This DNA could then be compared to DNA gathered from the workbench and from the remains found in the alleged Billy the Kid graves.

As expected, writers such as Nolan and others who claimed to be historians, who were defensive of the status quo and were also clearly concerned about their own reputations as "experts," have been reluctant to embrace a number of Sederwall's findings that contradict the legend. Though they have criticized said findings, none have come forth with any valid information or insight to dispute any of them in spite of invitations and challenges to do so.

The government of the state of New Mexico, from the office of the governor on down to city officials, has fought to keep the myths and legends of Billy the Kid and Pat Garrett alive, and initiated a number of attempts to thwart any quest for truth. Politics, in fact, have provided for an additional layer of drama and cover-up to the Billy the Kid story.

The experience of locating the workbench and the furniture from Maxwell's room generated an invitation to Sederwall to travel to Santa Fe for an "an important meeting" with then New Mexico governor Bill Richardson. Initially, Richardson made himself ubiquitous in the Billy the Kid investigations. It had become national news, and newspapers were eager for updates. Richardson, being a politician, appeared eager to be in front of the camera and to have the opportunity to expound to reporters. New Mexico legend Billy the Kid provided him with such opportunities.

During this time Sederwall was the mayor of Capitan, New Mexico, a town of fifteen hundred citizens twelve miles west of the town of Lincoln. At the same time he was also a reserve deputy with the Lincoln County Sheriff's Department. Accompanying Sederwall to Santa Fe was Lincoln County sheriff Tom Sullivan. On arrival, the two men were met by Billy Sparks, the governor's communications director. Following brief introductions, Sparks escorted Sederwall and Sullivan to the second floor of the capitol building and the office of Richardson. They had no sooner shaken hands with the governor when Sparks indicated that Sederwall needed to step outside the office with him. Sederwall and Sparks rode the elevator down to the parking garage because Sparks said he needed a cigarette.

Sparks appeared nervous and uncomfortable, and when Sederwall asked him what was going on, he said that Fred Nolan had called the governor. Nolan had long propagated the legend and was rather protective of his turf. Sparks told Sederwall that Nolan told the governor that the workbench that was found and examined was not the real one. He insisted to the governor that if the state acknowledged that this was the authentic workbench the politicos and the state would look like fools. Since Nolan had no way of knowing much of anything relative to the authenticity of the workbench, his defensive reaction suggested that he was irked that others were intruding into an area in which he considered himself an expert. Sparks then confessed that Richardson instructed him to have a talk with Sederwall about the situation.

Sederwall wanted to know how Nolan could have known about the discovery of the workbench six days after the fact and eight thousand miles away in England. Sparks claimed he didn't know, but Sederwall figured it out immediately. Present at the examination of the workbench was Paul Hutton, a history professor at the University of New Mexico and a Billy the Kid enthusiast. Hutton and Nolan were close; in the past they had appeared together at Billy the Kid–related events, where they supported each other's notions of history. Sederwall determined that Hutton likely contacted Nolan at the first opportunity and reported what was going on. It should also be pointed out that during this time Hutton served as Richardson's historical advisor relative to the Billy the Kid legend. The political bed was beginning to get crowded with elected politicians, governmental appointees and employees, and their sycophants.

Sparks informed Sederwall that his investigations had "a lot of people's nerves on edge," that Fort Sumner officials were running in circles worried that his findings were going to ruin their cash cow. A significant percentage of Fort Sumner's income, it was claimed, came from tourism related to Billy the Kid, specifically his nearby alleged gravesite adjacent to a tourist-oriented shop offering a number of Billy the Kid–related doodads for sale. Sparks explained that the governor's phones were ringing constantly, with callers hot with pressure "to rein you cowboys in before it gets out of hand." Sparks said that Raymond Lopez, the Fort Sumner mayor, had referred to Sederwall and Sullivan as "low-life, inbred sons-of-bitches."

Sparks also confessed that people were worried about what might be discovered relative to the DNA found on the workbench. Being somewhat idealistic about politics at the time, Sederwall told Sparks that he thought the governor, being the chief executive officer of the state of New Mexico, would be interested in the truth.

Sparks responded that the governor's office had just assumed that Sederwall would drive around, ask some questions, talk to the newspapers, and proudly declare that everything associated with the Billy the Kid legend was correct. Now, said Sparks, the governor was concerned that the results of the DNA analysis "could ruin the Kid legend," and that this was "making people nervous as hell," and that "every other call is someone demanding we stop this investigation."

As Sederwall and Sparks conversed in the parking garage, it finally sunk in: Sederwall finally realized this issue was not about a search for the truth at all; this was about politics and money. Governor Richardson was not in the least bit concerned with the truth other than how it might upset his constituents and perhaps interfere with his future plans. Richardson resembled Pat Garrett in this approach.

Sparks then suggested that Sederwall change his focus by making an application for a pardon for Billy the Kid. A pardon for one of the county's most notorious outlaws more than one hundred years after the fact would make national headlines and get the governor's picture in the papers again. Sederwall smelled a rat and asked the communications director to level with him and tell him exactly what was going on. Sparks finally came clean. His answer: politics, plain and simple. Sparks informed Sederwall that his photograph and details about the ongoing investigation were showing up in "every paper on the planet." Sederwall was getting more publicity than Governor Richardson.

Sederwall pressed Sparks for more details. Pacing and nervous, the aide said there was concern in the state that the DNA tests might prove that the Kid was *not* killed by Pat Garrett. Sederwall informed Sparks that all that people really wanted was the truth. Sparks replied that what they wanted was "New Mexico's truth."

Sederwall asked Sparks what the governor wanted out of this. Sparks replied that he wanted to be president of the United States. Sparks, pacing more and growing excited, explained that the governor's office had figured on the Kid investigations being to his liking, making a big splash, and causing everyone to be happy. Sparks said the governor's attorney, Bill Robins III, would file for a pardon for the Kid using Sederwall's investigations; the governor would get a lot of ink; Sederwall could have some "cop fun"; and the state of New Mexico would pull down some significant tourist dollars. Then, said Sparks, Sederwall found the workbench and the DNA business had the potential to become a liability.

Sparks was aware of Sederwall's investigations into John Miller and William Henry Roberts as potential Billy the Kids. Miller was buried in Arizona, Roberts in Texas. Somebody, who may or may not be Billy the Kid, was allegedly buried in Fort Sumner. Sparks, a spokesman for the state government of New Mexico, then revealed something interesting to Sederwall: "We don't know where the Kid is buried."

Sparks said that he could not tell Sederwall that this problem needed to go away because that would be interfering with an investigation, "but," he said, "I do know how we need this to turn out."

Sederwall headed Sparks off and told him that he perceived that the aide was communicating to him that, as an investigator, he was doing a great job but now had to stop, that the governor wanted to be president of the United States, and that the Billy the Kid issue was causing him heartburn. Sparks told Sederwall that he was correct in his analysis. Sparks then told Sederwall that he was giving him a "heads-up because they are coming," that "they have you and Sullivan in their crosshairs and before this is over it's going to get nasty. You guys are going to feel the heat."

Sederwall found out later that Fort Sumner mayor Lopez wrote a letter to the governor requesting that Richardson put a stop to the investigation, stating that it called into question "the validity of our grave of Billy the Kid." The governor assured Lopez that there would be no exhumation.

Interestingly, Bill Robins III, Richardson's attorney, filed in Grant County District Court to exhume Catherine Antrim, the Kid's presumed mother. Robins wanted to obtain her DNA. Shortly after the ink dried on the petition, Fort Sumner mayor Lopez hurried to Silver City to beg officials to prevent Sederwall or anyone else from gaining access to Antrim's DNA. Lopez's fear was that Antrim's DNA would not match the DNA from the workbench.

That same evening a special meeting of the Silver City town council was called to discuss the matter. One of the council members posed the question: "Who cares if [Sederwall] gets Antrim's DNA?" In response, Councilman Steve May became apoplectic and shouted that Silver City might regret this if the DNA showed that Billy the Kid was not buried in New Mexico. He stated, "We could be shooting ourselves in the foot," referring to perceived potential loss of tourist dollars.

The following morning, the *Silver City Sun-News* ran an article with the headline LAWMEN FILE PETITION TO EXHUME BILLY THE KID'S MOM. The article quoted Councilman May as stating: "I think it could have a truly negative impact if that's not Billy the Kid over there . . . and I don't think there's anyone alive in this town that can really truly say that's Mrs. Antrim in that grave. . . . What if all this means . . . Roberts in Texas was Billy the Kid? Then Fort Sumner is dead. That's their only claim to fame."

For Sederwall, Councilman May's statement provided a tell. He was afraid that the Kid was not buried in New Mexico. Note that the prospect of learning the truth, indeed, the very concept of the truth, never entered into the Silver City council's discussion. It was all about money.

A hearing on the exhumation of Catherine Antrim was scheduled for January 6, 2004. After listening to opposition to the request from a number of lawyers, Judge Henry Quintero decided on a postponement until August. After thinking about the matter, and acting before August, Quintero ruled: "Only if the petitioners are successful in locating the Kid's burial site and collecting his DNA, may they again petition this court for a review of Catherine Antrim's matter." Quintero made the ruling knowing full well that Fort Sumner would never permit anyone to dig into the Kid's "official gravesite." Quintero knew that the plan was to check Antrim's DNA against that of Roberts, Miller, and the remains at Fort Sumner. If Sederwall proved where the Kid was buried, there would be no need to return to Quintero's court, which is the way the judge wanted it.

In an odd twist, Governor Richardson's attorney Bill Robins filed a petition in the Tenth Judicial District, State of New Mexico, De Baca County, for the "Exhumation of Billy the Kid's remains" at Fort Sumner. Sederwall was beginning to wonder if Robins and Richardson ever talked to each other. If they did, and the governor was in on this, something suspicious was afoot.

Three days before the hearing, Billy Sparks called Sederwall and requested that he drop the motion to dig in Fort Sumner. Sederwall explained that he did not file the motion in the first place, that Robins did. Sparks said that Robins indeed filed the motion but did so using Sederwall's name, as well as Tom Sullivan's. Sparks said the motion could not be stopped without permission from the two lawmen.

Sederwall told Sparks that he had reason to believe that Billy the Kid was not buried in Fort Sumner. Sederwall posed the question to Sparks: "You know the Kid's not buried in Fort Sumner, don't you?" Sparks would not answer. Highly nervous, he said, "Help me out here, Steve."

After hanging up with Sparks, Sederwall called Robins and gave him permission to withdraw the motion. Sederwall learned later that Fort Sumner politicos threw a party on hearing the news. It all made him wonder why there was so much resistance to a quest for the truth. And then he found out: *There is no body under the Billy the Kid headstone at Fort Sumner.*

During the early phases of Sederwall's investigations, when Richardson thought he could get some political mileage out it, the governor assigned the state medical investigators office to the case. Sederwall was in conversation with this office almost daily. After listening to Sederwall lay out his theories and plans, state medical investigator Dr. Debra Komar traveled to Fort Sumner to examine what the state road signs proclaimed to be the "Official Grave of Billy the Kid."

After Komar performed her investigation at Fort Sumner, she traveled to Prescott, Arizona, to evaluate the remains of John Miller. Understandably, Sederwall was anxious to learn what Komar found out. Following her return, he made several calls to her office but was always told she was busy, tied up, or out of the office. Sederwall left several messages, but though a significant amount of time had elapsed, Komar never returned any of them.

It was apparent that Komar found something in Fort Sumner, or Prescott, or both, and that whatever it was, the state of New Mexico wanted it covered up. All communications between Sederwall and the medical investigators office were shut down. This left little doubt that the state officials had discovered something they did not want the public to know about.

Sederwall suspected interference from higher levels of state government, but he wanted answers. On January 20, 2004, Komar appeared in court in response to a subpoena. She was placed under oath and required to provide a deposition. She admitted that her investigation "on behalf of the State of New Mexico" took her to the Fort Sumner cemetery. She noted that Fort Sumner officials were upset about this. Komar was asked: "Were you able to determine whether there was a grave outline in the area of the purported site of Billy the Kid's grave?"

Komar replied, "Yes, we found it," She stated that she was able to pinpoint the grave believed by many to be that of the Kid and advertised as such by the state of New Mexico. As the Kid's companions Charlie Bowdre and Tom Folliard were purported to be buried alongside the outlaw, Komar was asked, "Were you able to determine how many graves were located in that vicinity?" She said no, and explained that "because we were not well received at Fort Sumner, [the methodology] was not done to the full extent that I would have done."

While under oath, Komar was asked if she had ever contacted Sederwall after returning from Prescott in response to the numerous messages he left. She replied, "I was not allowed to."

Sederwall wanted to know what Komar had discovered, but her attorney would not permit her to speak of it. Later Sederwall filed an Open Records Act request to the medical investigators office seeking the information found by Komar. The reply stated: "Dr. Komar, a faculty member of the University of New Mexico, and constitutes her intellectual property under federal copyright law and the University of New Mexico's Intellectual Property Policy."

This letter represented another tell. Reading between the lines, Sederwall deduced that Komar found something that would negate the legend of Billy the Kid if the information were released.

While under oath Komar was asked: "You don't think Billy the Kid is buried at Fort Sumner, do you?" Komar, who on the stand represented the medical investigators office of the state of New Mexico, replied, "I don't know. I have reason to suspect perhaps not."

The question remains: What, if anything, did Komar find beneath the Kid's headstone, and why was the information being withheld? The answer to that question may have been learned seven months earlier. Sederwall discovered that on June 17, 2003, David Bailey, an ex-mayor of Fort Sumner, provided the information that officials of Fort Sumner, as well as the state of New Mexico, wanted kept secret. On that day Bailey told De Baca County sheriff Gary Graves that he, the sheriff, had to do something to stop Sederwall's investigation because "we know what's in that grave."

What information related to the alleged grave of Billy the Kid could Bailey possibly have? As Sederwall subsequently learned, weeks earlier Bailey and a companion took it upon themselves to travel to the location of the grave of Billy the Kid, breach the fence that enclosed it, and conduct an excavation. When they had completed their task, they were concerned about the obvious dig marks, so they shoveled into other graves nearby to make it appear to be the work of vandals.

What did they find? *Nothing.* There were no remains under the headstone denoting the grave of Billy the Kid.

Chapter Twenty

Conclusion

The historians got it wrong. The entire Billy the Kid story many of us grew up with is legend. It is a fine legend, one filled with adventure, romance, derring-do, and tragedy. It is a legend that had, and has, a firm grip on the American—yea, the world—public, one that has generated over a thousand books, seventy-five films, countless articles, and even a Broadway play. But it is not the truth.

Someone once said that the American public, when confronted with a choice between the myth and the truth, will generally choose the myth. This is understandable. The Billy the Kid myth, enduring as it is and has been, has become part of our consciousness. We wrap ourselves around the myth, embrace it, for that myth is what we know, and we don't want to turn loose of it. We don't want to be told that what we have always believed is not true. Norman Pago wrote, "If enough people believe in a myth it can have the power of truth."

The historians and writers who have traded on the legend and myth of Billy the Kid over the past decades have demonstrated little interest in, or ability to encounter, the truth. The truth was always there, but it was covered over and hidden by layers of the legend. It took someone on a quest for truth, someone like Steve Sederwall, someone with the necessary skill, experience, and patience to peel back those layers and uncover what was always there but undiscovered.

More often than not, in the research of century-old events that have been catapulted into legend via books, articles, movies, and more, the truth has been rendered difficult to locate, to uncover. Finding the truth often requires deep focus and hard work. To their everlasting embarrassment and disgrace, many of the historians and writers concerned with Billy the Kid did not invest sufficient time and energy into searching for the truth, but contented themselves with simply repeating one another. When one constructs an evolutionary chart of the process and progress of the Billy the Kid legend from its origins down to the present day, one finds that all of the threads eventually connect back to *The Authentic Life of Billy the Kid*, the book that bears Pat Garrett's name as the author, though it has become clear that he did not write much, if any, of it. Most of the contents can be ascribed to Garrett's ghostwriter, Ashmon Upson. The errors, misstatements, and at times deliberate lies encountered in this publication have all been pointed out over the years and are numerous. A thorough examination of these two men—Garrett and Upson—reveals that neither of them possessed a shred of credibility and that they appeared reluctant to treat the truth with the respect and dignity it deserved. In spite of this, the book has been the original source of virtually all of the misinformation put forth about the outlaw Billy the Kid.

A number of books have been released in recent years with "new" findings and interpretations that have clearly pointed out to us that history is not always correct. One of the earliest of these was Dee Brown's *Bury My Heart at Wounded Knee*, wherein, as a result of his research and investigation, Brown revealed to us that most of the "valiant" and "courageous" military victories over the American Indians amounted to little more than wholesale massacres of old men, women, and children accompanied by the rape, mutilation, and slaughter of unarmed and unresisting residents. Today, this would be termed "terrorism." These so-called heroic victories over recalcitrant and defenseless Indians were lies perpetuated by the United States government.

There are dozens more examples, and the accepted history associated with Billy the Kid is one of them. Many people will reject the truth, preferring to retain the legend. The historians have criticized and condemned truths that conflict with their versions of what happened, and they will continue to do so because to accept, or even consider, a new truth or theory that is in opposition to their long-occupied position would be tantamount to admitting they were wrong. They won't do that. For them it is more about ego and maintaining their perception of status than it is about truth. Attempts on the part of a number of Billy the Kid historians and writers, as well as the state of New Mexico, to suppress the truth are a matter of record.

The historians will fade away to be replaced by others, hopefully men and women with open minds and with no intentions of erecting barriers. Politicians will likewise depart, though hope for honesty and integrity in that arena has long proven to be futile. Years will roll on, and Steve Sederwall, and others like him, will turn to dust. The truth he uncovered, however, will remain, will endure.

ACKNOWLEDGMENTS

PROPER INVESTIGATIVE WORK—FROM THE SEARCH FOR AND collection of evidence and clues to developing conclusions—is more often than not a team effort. A number of interested and skilled individuals were involved in deriving the information presented in this book. They include Thomas Boring, David A. Brewer, John Cooper, Jud Cooper, Tom Darrah, Gary Graves, Mike Haag, Ron Hadley, Dr. Henry Lee, Lonnie Lippmann, Wes Owen, Mike Perez, Rick Staub, Tom Sullivan, Dale Tunnell, Dave Turk, and John Wilson.

Over a considerable period of time, Steve Sederwall painstakingly collected, organized, and analyzed data and findings, compiling in-depth reports and summarizing conclusions. The results were shared with other investigators, historians, and Billy the Kid enthusiasts and their comments invited.

After Sederwall's findings were organized into manuscript form, subsequent drafts were subjected to Laurie Jameson, one of the country's top editors, who applied her expertise to the presentation.

SELECTED BIBLIOGRAPHY

Books

Airy, Helen. *Whatever Happened to Billy the Kid?* Santa Fe, N.M.: Sunstone Press, 1993.

Anaya, Paco. *I Buried Billy.* College Station, Tex.: Creative Publishing, 1991.

Angel, Frank Warner. *The Angel Report* ("Report on the Death of John H. Tunstall"). Washington: Records of the Department of Justice, 1878.

Ball, Eve. *Ma'am Jones of the Pecos.* Tucson: University of Arizona Press, 1980.

Barron, R. M. (ed.). *The Court of Inquiry of Lieutenant Colonel Dudley, Vol. One.* Edina, Mont.: Beaver's Pond Press, 1995.

Bell, Bob Boze. *The Illustrated Life and Times of Billy the Kid,* 2nd ed. Phoenix: Tri-Star—Boze Publications, 1996.

Brothers, May Hudson. *Billy the Kid, the Most Hated, the Most Loyal Outlaw New Mexico Ever Produced.* Farmington, N.M.: Hustler Press, 1949.

Brown, Dee. *Bury My Heart at Wounded Knee.* New York: Holt, Rinehart and Winston, 1970.

Burns, Walter Noble. *The Saga of Billy the Kid.* New York: Grossett and Dunlap, 1926.

Coe, George W. *Frontier Fighter.* Albuquerque: University of New Mexico Press, 1984.

Cook, Jim. *Lane of the Llano.* Boston: Little Brown and Company, 1936.

Dykes, J. C. *Billy the Kid: The Bibliography of a Legend.* Albuquerque: University of New Mexico Press, 1952.

Fulton, Maurice Garland. *History of the Lincoln County War.* Tucson: University of Arizona Press, 1997.

———. *Notes on Morton and Baker.* Tucson: University of Arizona Press, 1953.

———. *Roswell in its Early Years.* Roswell, N.M.: Hall-Poorbaugh Press, 1963.

Garrett, Patrick F. *The Authentic Life of Billy the Kid.* Norman: University of Oklahoma Press, 1954.

Gillette, James B. *Fugitive from Justice: The Notebook of Texas Ranger Sergeant James B. Gillette.* Austin, Tex.: State House Press, 1997.

———. *Six Years with the Texas Rangers.* Lincoln, Nebr.: Bison Press, 1976.

Glenn, Skelton. *Pat Garrett as I Knew Him on the Buffalo Range*. Robert N. Mullin Collection, J. Evetts Haley Memorial Library and History Center. No date.

Hoyt, Henry F. *A Frontier Doctor*. New York: Houghton Mifflin Co., 1929.

Jacobsen, Joel. *Such Men as Billy the Kid*. Lincoln: University of Nebraska Press, 1994.

Jameson, W. C. *Pat Garrett: The Man Behind the Badge*. Boulder, Colo.: Taylor Trade Publishing, 2015.

———. *Billy the Kid: The Lost Interviews*. Clearwater, Fla.: Garlic Press, 2012.

———. *Billy the Kid: Beyond the Grave*. Boulder, Colo.: Taylor Trade Publishing, 2005.

Kaldec, Robert F. *They "Knew" Billy the Kid: Interviews with Old-Time New Mexicans*. Santa Fe, N.M.: Ancient City Press, 1987.

Klassner, Lily. *My Childhood among Outlaws*. Tucson: University of Arizona Press, 1972.

Lake, Stewart. *The Frontier Marshall*.

McCarty, John L. *Maverick Town: The Story of Old Tascosa*. Norman: University of Oklahoma Press, 1946.

McCright, Grady E., and James H. Powell. *Jessie Evans: Lincoln County Badman*. College Station, Tex.: Creative Publishing Company, 1983.

Meadows, John P. *Pat Garrett and Billy the Kid as I Knew Them: Reminiscences of John P. Meadows*. Albuquerque: University of New Mexico Press, 2004.

Nolan, Frederick. *The West of Billy the Kid*. Norman: University of Oklahoma Press, 1998.

———. *The Lincoln County War: A Documentary History*. Norman: University of Oklahoma Press, 1992.

Poe, John W. *The Death of Billy the Kid*. Boston: Houghton Mifflin Co., 1933.

Poe, Sophie A. *Buckboard Days*. Albuquerque: University of New Mexico Press, 1981.

Polk, C. W. *The Capture of Billy the Kid* (edited by James H. Earle). College Station, Tex.: Creative Publishing, 1988.

Prassell, Frank Richard. *The Great American Outlaw*. Norman: University of Oklahoma Press, 1993.

Rasch, Phillip J. *Trailing Billy the Kid*. Laramie, Wyo.: National Association for Outlaw and Lawman History, Inc., 1995.

Shinkle, James D. *Martin V. Corn, Early Roswell Pioneer*. Roswell, N.M.: Hall-Poorbaugh Press, 1972.

Shipman, Jack. "Brief career of Tom O'Folliard, Billy the Kid's partner." *Voice of the Mexican Border*, 1934. Robert N. Mullin Collection.

Shipman, O. L. *Letters Past and Present*. Self-published, 1934. Robert N. Mullin Collection.

Siringo, Charles A. *History of Billy the Kid*. Albuquerque: University of New Mexico Press, 1956.

Tatum, Stephen. *Inventing Billy the Kid: Visions of the Outlaw 1881-1981*. Albuquerque: University of New Mexico Press, 1982.
Turk, David S. *Blackwater Draw*. Santa Fe, N.M.: Sunstone Press, 2011.
Tuska, Jon. *Billy the Kid: His Life and Legend*. Albuquerque: University of New Mexico Press, 1994.
Utley, Robert M. *Billy the Kid: A Short and Violent Life*. Lincoln: University of Nebraska Press, 1989.
——— (ed.). *Maurice G. Fulton's History of the Lincoln County War*. Tucson: University of Arizona Press, 1968.
Walker, Dale L. *The Calamity Papers*. New York: Forge, 2004.
———. *Legends and Lies: Great Mysteries of the American West*. New York: Forge, 1997.
———. *C. L. Sonnichsen: Grassroots Historian*. El Paso: Texas Western Press, 1972.

Diary

Dr. Taylor F. Ealy.

Interviews

Bede, George. Federal Writers Project, National Archives, Washington.
Corn, Robert. 10 June 1938. WPA Federal Writers Project, National Archives, Washington.
Ealy, James. Interview by J. Evetts Haley, 27 September 1927. J. Evetts Haley Collection, Midland, Tex.
Farmer, Sam. 25 July 1938. WPA Federal Writers Project, Library of Congress, Manuscript Division, Washington.
Lesnett (no first name indicated). 30 September 1937. Federal Writers Project, National Archives, Washington.
Marley, Mary Corn. 17 April 1938. Federal Writers Project, Library of Congress, Manuscript Division, Washington, DC.
Salazar, Margarita. Interview by José Salazar, 28 November 1977. Lincoln County Historical Society Publications, Hondo, N.M.
Trujillo, Francisco. Interview by Edith Crawford, 1937. National Archives, Washington.

Letters

Boylan, John, to Hiram M. Dow. 25 July 1963.
Brazel, Manuel, to Manuel Abreau. 13 February 1892.
Cummins, Ben M. 20 November 1997.
Ealy, Taylor, to Sheldon Jackson. 13 August 1878.
East, James H., to Judge William H. Burgess. 20 May 1926. Fulton Collection, Tucson, Ariz.
East, James H., to Charlie Siringo. 1 May 1920.

Fuiginita, Laura C., to Dale L. Tunnel. 2 June 2005.
Gillette, James B., to E. A. Brimstool. 21 February 1923. Brimstool Collection, Center for American History, University of Texas at Austin.
"Las Cruces Thirty-Four," from a man known only as Max. 5 March 1879.
Leverson, M. R., to President Rutherford B. Hayes. 2 April 1881. National Archives, Washington.
Leverson, M. R., to John Sherman Jr. 20 March 1878. National Archives.
Lopez, Raymond, to New Mexico governor Bill Richardson. 1 October 2003.
Mitchell, B. W., to James A. Tomlinson. 30 April 1881. Rio Grande Historical Collection, New Mexico State University Library, Las Cruces.
Morton, W. S., to H. H. Marshall. 1878.
Tomlinson, James A., to Justice of the Peace Jesus Lueras. 29 April 1881.
Wallace, Lew, to James B. Gillette. Lew Wallace Collection, William Henry Smith Memorial Library, Indiana Historical Society, Indianapolis.

Newspapers

"Brockway's Forged Bonds," *New York Times*, 6 May 6 1882.
Carrizozo Outlook, Carrizozo, N.M., 3 April 1936.
Daily Optic, Las Vegas, N.M., 8 December 1879.
Drummond, A. L. "True Detective Stories: A Genius Who Went Wrong," *New York Herald*, 20 December 1908.
Jameson, W. C. "Who Was Billy the Kid?" *NOLA Quarterly*, October-December 1998, pp. 17, 18, 20.
Las Vegas Gazette, Las Vegas, N.M., 4 May 1878, 29 December 1880, 12 May 1881.
Lincoln County Leader, White Oaks, N.M., 15 January 1890. Article by Gottfried Gauss.
Mesilla Valley Gazette, Mesilla, N.M., 23 April 1878, 4 May 1878.
New Mexican, Santa Fe, 21 May 1880.
New York Times, 6 May 1882.
"Old Counterfeiters Caught," *New York Times*, 24 October 1880.
Redfield, Georgia B. "Two Who Knew Billy the Kid Recall Exploits of Outlaw," *El Paso Times*, El Paso, Tex., 7 August 1955.
Sun News, Silver City, N.M., 11 October 2003.
White Oaks Leader, 15 January 1890.

Reports

Angel Report, Department of Justice, File No. 44-4-8-3. National Archives, Washington.
Annual Report of the Secret Service Division of the United States Treasury Department, ending 30 June 1881. National Archives.
Blazer, A. N., to Maurice G. Fulton. 10 April 1930. Fulton Collection.

Blazer, A. N., to Maurice G. Fulton. 24 April 1931. Fulton Collection, University of Arizona, Tucson.

Blazer, A. N., to Maurice G. Fulton. 27 April 1937.

Boring, Thomas. Report on the 45-60. Special provided to Steve Sederwall.

Boring, Thomas. Supplemental Report for Lincoln County Sheriff's Case #2003-274. 28 June 2006.

Brewer, David A. Supplemental Report: Involuntary Neuromuscular Response and Stress. Provided to Steve Sederwall, 15 June 2004.

Brooks, James L. Evaluation Report on Secret Service Operatives. 26 September 1877. National Archives.

Caperton, Thomas J. Historic Structure Report, Lincoln State Monument, New Mexico. 1983. State of New Mexico, Santa Fe.

Commissioner of General Land Office's Report, 1869.

Commissioner of General Land Office's Report, 1872.

Daily Report of District Chief Wallace W. Hall of the Secret Service. 19 May 1880. National Archives.

Daily Report of District Chief Wallace W. Hall of the Secret Service. 4 August 1880. National Archives.

Daily Report of District Chief Wallace W. Hall of the Secret Service. 24 February 1881. National Archives.

Daily Report of District Chief Wallace W. Hall of the Secret Service. 26 February 1881. National Archives.

Daily Report of District Chief Wallace W. Hall of the Secret Service. 11 October 1881. National Archives.

Daily Report of District Chief Wallace W. Hall of the Secret Service. 9 May 1882. National Archives.

Daily Report of District Chief Wallace W. Hall to Chief Brooks. 19 May 1882. National Archives.

Daily Report of District Chief Wallace W. Hall of the Secret Service. 27 May 1882. National Archives.

Daily Report of Azariah Wild, Secret Service Operative, to Chief Brooks. 28 October 1880. National Archives.

Daily Report of Azariah Wild, Secret Service Operative, to Chief Brooks. 10 November 1880. National Archives.

Daily Report of Azariah Wild, Secret Service Operative, to Chief Brooks. 3 January 1881. National Archives.

Daily Report of Azariah Wild, Secret Service Operative, to Chief Brooks. 4 October 1881. National Archives.

Daily Report of Azariah Wild, Secret Service Operative, to Chief Brooks. 16 October 1881. National Archives.

Daily Report of Chief James Brooks of the United States Secret Service. 30 November 1880. National Archives.

Daily Report of Patrick Tyrell, United States Secret Service. 8 July 1881. National Archives.

Deposition of Dr. Debra Komar, New Mexico Medical Investigator, Silver City, New Mexico. 20 January 2004.

Dills, Lucius. Billy the Kid Review and Appraisal. Robert N. Mullin Collection, Haley Memorial Library and History Center, Midland, Tex.

Garrett, Pat F. Administrative report for the estate of Robert Olinger. Lincoln County Court Records, Lincoln County, N.M.

Haag, Michael G. Firearm and Tool Mark Section Report. 26 June 2006. Metropolitan Forensic Science Center, Albuquerque, N.M.

Lee, Dr. Henry. Forensic Examination Report (Lincoln County Courthouse). 22 May 2004.

Lee, Dr. Henry. Forensic Examination Report (Examination of Furniture from Pete Maxwell's of July 15, 1881). 22 May 2004.

Lincoln County Commissioners Records. 4 April 1881.

Lincoln County Mining Records. Lincoln County, New Mexico County Courthouse.

New Mexico Bar Association Disciplinary Board Ref. #26036.

Possessions of Sheriff Brady. 1 April 1878. County of Lincoln, Territory of New Mexico. Michael Perez Collection.

Prescott Police Department Case #06-12767. Prescott, Ariz.

Probate File for Billy Morton. Lincoln County Courthouse, Carrizozo, N.M.

Record Group, Office of Quartermaster General Consolidated Correspondence File, 1794-1915, Box 1093. National Archives.

Salazar, Yginio, statement to Raphaela Pryor. Robert Mullin Collection, Haley Memorial Library and History Center, Midland, Tex.

Secret Service New Orleans Operator Azariah Wild's Daily Report to Chief Brooks. 12 June 1880. National Archives.

Secret Service New Orleans Operative Azariah Wild's Daily Report to Chief Brooks. 6 October 1881. National Archives.

Secret Service New Orleans Operator Azariah Wild's Daily Report to Chief Brooks. 11 June 1880. National Archives.

Smith, J. Vernon. Lucien B. Maxwell's House. 15 April 1935. WPA Federal Writers Project. National Archives.

Tenth Judicial District, State of New Mexico, DeBaca County, Case #CV-04-00005.

The United States of America v. William Wilson, National Archives, Rocky Mountain Region Records, Broomfield, Colo.

1860 Census. Charlotte County, Virginia.

1880 Census. Lincoln County, New Mexico.

Additional

Archival Records. Texas Ranger Hall of Fame, Waco, Tex.

INDEX